# Career Headline

## Laid Off & Loving It For 2010

- Outsourced Accountant Uses Social Media to Get A New Gig

- Former Software Company Exec Becomes a Business Advisor

- Downsized Exec Tweets For Success in Financial Services

- Severed Purchasing Agent Profits From His Obsession

- Laid-Off Librarian Is Passionate About Selling Data

- Early Retiree Principal Becomes An Event Planner

- Retired Air Force Major Creates His Own Job

- Burned-Out Nurse Moves Beyond Healthcare

- Forced-Out CEO Becomes A Headhunter

These and other career transitions are just ahead...

# *Laid Off & Loving It For 2010*

## Rebuilding Your Career or Small Business with Social Media's Help

Paul David Madsen

**AmericasJobCoach.com**

*Since 2001*

**growmedia.com**
**Omaha, Nebraska**
**U.S.A.**

# Laid Off & Loving It For 2010
## Rebuilding Your Career or Small
## Business with Social Media's Help

Published by:
**growmedia.com**
**Omaha, NE U.S.A.**
**www.growmedia.com**

Book design: Patricia Rasch /bookandcoverdesign.com

Copyright © 2009 by Paul David Madsen /growmedia.com
Library of Congress Cataloging-in-Publication Data:
Madsen, Paul David.
  **Laid Off & Loving It For 2010**
  Rebuilding Your Career or Small Business with Social Media's Help
  Paul David Madsen
  Includes Biographical references
  **ISBN:** 9780971383616
  1. Careers. 2. Employment 3. Small Business
  II. Title: Laid Off & Loving It For 2010 *Rebuilding Your Career or Small Business with Social Media's Help*
  **Library of Congress Control Number: 2009907560**

# Why This Book Can Help You

For most people, a career crisis can be among the most stressful of life events. Finances and self-esteem are bruised and bloodied. The pressure builds because we live in a changing world. Today, the search for relevant answers to career questions and dilemmas through the use of conventional wisdom and traditional solutions often leads to disappointment. What to do?

We attempt to navigate the ladder of success in an age when job security is nothing more than illusion. Like a mirage in the desert, positions and careers vanish with little notice. The reality of work life today is that security and risk have become so compressed that it's difficult to recognize one from the other.

In this volatile environment, we must focus on what we *can* control. Making appropriate occupational choices is fundamental to success, but frequently difficult. Whether laid off or unhappily employed, you stand at the crossroads of two divergent journeys. One road is traditional and well worn, the other progressive, sophisticated and personal. Choosing the first highway might get you a job. Venturing down the road less traveled can provide fulfillment and meaning.

You have taken the customary route before...resumes, cover letters, networking, job fairs, online searches, and phone calls. You know when you "arrive" because you end up with a job offer, but you are not sure how you got there *or even if you want to be there.*

There is nothing mystical or obscure about an alternate route, but it does require plans and processes that are not self-evident. To implement this new strategy, you will need a guide. My strong recommendation is Career Coach, Headhunter, and Employment Specialist Paul David Madsen, C.P.C.

Mr. Madsen is supremely qualified for the task. I first crossed paths with Paul in the early days of our careers when we were employed at an executive search firm. Even then, it was clear that Paul had great enthusiasm for the employment services sector. Specifically, it was clear then, as it is now, that Paul has both a deep passion and skill for enabling the occupational successes of others.

Paul has gained a diverse, in-depth understanding of the employment landscape. Years of executive recruiting, contract placement, out-placement and career coaching experience give Paul insight and perspective. He has personally been involved with the successful career transitions of hundreds of job seekers, career changers, seminar attendees, and individual coaching clients.

Libraries are laden with stuffy "How To" books that are rarely read. Laid Off & Loving It! though, teaches without being preachy or academic. Through a series of concise, inspirational narratives, you will learn how others like you have solved their own career crises. Later, you are provided with a nuts-and-bolts framework for forward movement in your own exciting occupational journey.

Will your business or job make something for you or will it make something of you? The relevance and value of achieving a thing is not so much in attainment of the goal, but rather in what we must become to make it happen. What do you want to become? My friend Paul David Madsen's book will empower you to define and obtain YOUR occupational desires.

Curt McLey, CPC
CEO, Harrison Moore, Inc.
& Long-Time Radio Personality

# How Are YOU Affected?

Everyone who performs work will encounter changes in their work life. Today's economy is a volatile mix of moving parts creating job instability unseen in a generation. In June 2009 the US Bureau of Labor reported a 9.5 percent unemployment rate for a total of **14.7 MILLION unemployed** people in the USA. This represents the highest rate in over 25 years. That's well over the population of the entire state of Pennsylvania! There are predictions of double digit unemployment into 2010 and perhaps beyond. We all hope some experts are wrong when they say US business conditions may never again return to the "Roaring 1990s" status. Today's conditions affect nearly everyone whether they are employed or unemployed.

I have never seen more people **over the age of 50** who are on the job hunt. At that age people are very interested in preserving their former incomes and lifestyles. But this global economy is having a drastic effect on them and other groups as well. Millions of workers are underpaid, under-challenged, restless, bored, and nervous about their future. They may hate their jobs, their career fields, or even their bosses but they are just trying to hang on.

Charles Darwin stated, "It is not the strongest of the

species that survives, nor the most intelligent that survives. It is the one that is the most adaptable to change." Read that again and ask yourself how adaptable to change you are being in your current career situation.

Use this book to survive and adapt. Together let's block some of the punches the workplace might be throwing at you. I want to help you respond to this street fight with some counterpunches which help you achieve your sustainable income or career. How you react now could determine your vocational survival.

Adaptability is critical because to keep income-producing work today, we are competing against people from across the street, from across the state, and from across the globe. Technology, globalization trade deficits, governmental oversight or a lack of that, Wall Street Gone Wild, sex, age, and race discrimination, layoffs, downsizing, and off-shoring all affect employers and the people they employ or contract with.

"Medical Tourism" exemplifies our changing world. A web site of an India-based conglomerate states a heart valve replacement surgery in the USA can cost $200,000. They "sell" theirs for only $10,000 in US dollars—but wait there's more! For that price they throw in round trip airfare, lodging with concierge/interpreter service, and customized site-seeing. You can get a free online quote for a hip replacement faster than you can drive to your local orthopedic surgeon's office! The point is this: In today's workplace, doctors, lawyers, and you and I must build Buoyant and Branded Skills. If we don't, our career might sink.

The narratives in this book chronicle how people like you handled a wide variety of workplace transitions. The lessons these people demonstrate arise from the 25,000+

people I have personally interviewed while working as a career strategist for over two decades. I have directly placed hundreds of people in better jobs in addition to coaching many more hundreds in seminars, classes, one-on-one sessions, etc. This input plus my own strategic inclinations form the backdrop for this book. Lastly, I have personally used many of the strategies in this book due to an absurd number of separations from my former employers.

A paraphrase of a popular saying is "insanity is when you do the same thing over and over and expect a different result." Does that apply to your career transition? At this point in your career and in the current economic conditions, I recommend you stay open, stay adaptable, and consider most options.

Thanks for inviting me to be a part of your professional journey. I look forward to hearing about how YOU achieved your vocational victory!

Paul David Madsen
America's Job Coach
June 2009

The greatest good you can
do for another is not just
to share your riches, but to
reveal to him, *his own.*

Benjamin Disreali

# Table of Contents

# Section 1

# Life in the Trenches

# 1

# Changing Uses Changes Value

## CEO Harry Now Hunts Heads

Harry the CEO had been with his firm for 19 years prior to being laid off. He started with the budding telemarketing company in the 1980s right after earning his Bachelor Degree in Business Administration.

The company was very young and one of the first dozen or so companies in the country that provided external, in-bound customer service for its clients as well as direct response order fulfillment for TV, radio or print advertising.

The concept of outsourcing the functions of call centers and customer service was brand new back when Harry joined the fledgling company. His job was to sell the company's services to businesses that wished to not have to hire and build their own call centers and telemarketing functions. It was a concept whose time had come.

He went on to enjoy a great climb to the top in this "early adaptor" company. That early-mover advantage enabled the company to grow to over 2,800 employees in fourteen call centers in six states. Quite a change from the time when firm had just sixty-two employees on board when Harry signed on. Phone-based, inbound sales and customer support were becoming the business norm for many corporations who outsourced these functions to companies like Harry's. And he was smart enough to ride that wave.

Harry proved adept at bringing in new, high-profile clients, projects and accounts so his promotion to sales manager was logical. He completed his evening/weekend MBA program at a local, prestigious university. That effort was a strain on his job and his young family but he pulled it off after 3 years of late night work. He made sure several senior level people at his employer knew that he accomplished this "I'm on the way up" kind of degree. He'd casually talk about his courses and case studies with anyone of influence who would listen. He invited every one of the officers and executives at his growing company to his graduation.

After closing even more new major accounts, and adeptly playing company politics, Harry was promoted to VP of Sales. Harry's passion for the company ran deep and his accomplishments enabled him to have access to the eclectic company founder. They would golf and occasionally attend horse racing events together, a passion of the founder.

Harry's sales staff continued to thrive in the emerging market space of outsourced teleservices. More technical innovations were creating growth opportunities and Harry's strategic side thrived in what became the roaring 90's. His sales staff had a deep sense of belonging and community. They'd voluntarily put in long, long hours in order to maintain the festive, competitive, "we're all in this together and going places" type of feel. Sales grew as did profitability.

The company had become positioned for an Initial Public Offering of its stock and that process went well. Harry's MBA

2

studies showed him case studies of how employees who were in the right place at the right time had earned stock options. His access to the founder gave Harry the forum to have secured a significant number of these gems prior to the IPO. The firm's initial offering was a success due to their status as the biggest player in their industry of interactive customer service and sales. Harry's net worth approached seven figures on paper.

The up and coming executives in Harry's MBA program agreed to his requests for mentoring. They had encouraged him to shore up his weaknesses and change his employer's "seat of the pants" style and pattern it more on established business models. This all helped Harry's rising star and his influence and he began to impact departments beyond his own sales organization.

His sales group was now a national team and was nearly worshipped by most of the senior executives. One or two men at that level resented Harry's "golden child" status, thinking that anyone could sell a lot of clients during those economic times. They felt technology or operations were the real worker bees of the company. Harry worked about seventy-five hours a week, traveled extensively to hire and support his sales executives and began earning more time at the table of the company's regular Friday morning senior executive meetings. At these meetings his ideas began to enhance operations, finance, HR, and production divisions, helping him to raise his profile even more.

As the founder lost interest in running the day-to-day operations, Harry's name naturally surfaced as a replacement. He was not surprisingly appointed President of one of the separate operating companies. The CEO title for that group followed not too long afterward. The founder who was the largest stockholder, hung around as Chairman of the Board and kept 3 President/CEOs of his operating companies reporting to him. Harry ran the biggest of those operating companies.

Harry enjoyed a salary and bonuses in the mid six figures, stock incentives, travel perks and a country club membership at the city's most prestigious club. He savored the admiration of his peers, the national recognition, and this ultimate endorsement of his hard work and proven expertise. And yet he remained relatively humble throughout the process.

It was fun for Harry to see how doors opened for him due to his new title. He had maintained and managed his own rapidly growing personal contacts database since he was a entry-level salesman. That list now grew even more rapidly. His automated data base totaled about 4,000 contacts that he had personally made across his career. And he had kept track of all their contact information.

As the top dog, Harry made key staffing actions and put his personal stamp on the operation. Under this leadership, the company continued to chug away, earning steady profits and always keeping an eye toward market share growth and domination.

After five years as CEO, Harry's market changed. The Internet became the new buzzword in the direct marketing world. Public sentiment against telemarketing was growing and Congress passed restrictive 'Do Not Call" laws and programs. Wall Street analysts eventually punished Harry's firm for not being ahead of the curve on the Internet and for not being diverse enough when Congress was spinning its punitive web. The company's stock tanked.

The founder's nephew was on the board of directors. He

talked endlessly about the "New Net Economy." With an eye on Harry's job, he eventually persuaded the board to dump their "relic" of a CEO. Years of steady profits meant nothing in the face of amazing Internet IPO stories. The once golden child named Harry became the ultimate fall guy right as the dot com bubble burst. The board had wanted part of the exciting Internet exuberance stories reiterated by a relative of the founder. It didn't seem to matter much that the nephew had no history of career success.

Harry's tenure was known for simply old fashioned telephone work on which the firm had been founded. Not yet forty years old, Harry was considered a "has been" and on the street. His severance package equaled one year of pay of his former cash compensation.

Bitter at first, Harry moped around for nearly a month before getting active. He traveled, golfed, and began extensive research. And he was finally able to keep his dates with his special friend, Barb.

After four months Harry had nearly reached his limit in research and he was amused by the two job interviews he accepted. They had been lined up through two niche industry headhunters he had come to know over the years. The interviews were mostly courtesy interviews at competitors and jobs were junior to his former position and status.

After one of the interviews, the former CEO became intrigued with the headhunter's profession. He learned how success in that field was based on one's ability to network and make introductions of the right players to each other at the right time.

Harry had the sales ability and contacts—he was already considered one of the industry's best connected professionals. In his sales work he had golfed with the VPs and CEOs of many companies in the mid market to enterprise-level space. While he was on his way up, many of the Fortune 1000 had become clients of Harry's former employer. This was in no small part due to Harry's strong abilities and strengths of Woo and persuasion.

ॐ

The headhunter named Kyle told Harry of his own pending retirement.

"Kyle," Harry said, "You are way too young to retire." Kyle's reply was, "Harry, I have worked many years as a recruiter. The field has been very good to me so I'm well positioned to be able to pursue my dream of becoming a club pro and living near my grandkids." Harry thought it sounded like a great plan but coerced Kyle to first spend a couple of weeks showing Harry the ropes of the industry he was leaving. Harry paid Kyle a generous consulting fee and Kyle said he was only a phone call away if the student ever needed more coaching.

Harry elected to start his own solo recruiting practice rather than be part of an established political firm. He didn't want to be told what clients he could or could not call on and which candidates he could or could not consider as his own. He knew he could learn from others, but also felt confident with Kyle's coaching and insights. Harry had also been on the other side of the desk with headhunters for many years.

He relished his new small but luxurious office near his home. Some executive recruiters worked out of their homes but Harry chose an executive center so he'd be around other professionals and better able to separate his work from his home life.

He outfitted his office with fine quality, used furnishings.

He planned on very little foot traffic so he didn't need a receptionist, support staff or auspicious furniture. Most of his dealings with live people were going to be at industry meetings, their offices, or in social venues. His back office bookkeeping and similar functions were all outsourced so he planned to have no employees, payroll, or human resource management issues. It was nice not to have no reports! His former coworkers at the teleservices firm were jealous of Harry's short 45 hour work weeks and his lack of staff or board issues.

Harry established a routine of phoning dozens of his industry contacts each day. He didn't worry about cold calls to new potential clients or candidates. Due to his severance package and many years of living within his means, he was not desperate or in a rush. Utilizing his personal database, Harry felt like the old days when he was a young account executive. Only this time, he possessed the "rolodex to die for." Hundreds of people knew Harry.

Harry's goal was to place four six-figure, C-Level executives in his first year. And he reached it. Three of the four were candidates he knew in the industry. One was a former employee of Harry's prior employer. All were placed at competitors of Harry's old firm where Harry had previous relationships.

Harry did not steal any talent from his former employer although many of his old team begged him to help them find new jobs. He honored his non-compete, non-disclosure and non-solicitation agreements to the letter.

Harry's average placement fee was $41,000 so his first year gross revenue did not come close to matching his former comp plan. But with his small office expenses he was on his way to "doing OK" as he called it.

When he got started many years ago in the teleservices industry, he was entry level. All through his fast-track career he had managed to keep his head and not spend big. His home and lifestyle were upscale but relatively modest. He saw some of his peers get big salaries and comp plans and start doing lots of heavy personal spending. When the downturns hit, they were hurting. But not Harry—he avoided debt as much as possible and that allowed him to get by on the money he earned in his new recruiting practice.

Now Harry selects his own hours and projects. He feels poised to grow revenues by at least 50% in his second full year. He became engaged to Barbara instead of being married to his former employer. Except for the big contract wins which raised lots of boats back at his old firm, Harry rarely misses the pressure, stress and politics of his former days as a CEO.

ले॰

To see web sites which helped Harry,
please go to **www.growmedia.com**.

# 2

# Use Social Networking to Succeed

## Accountant Amy Links In

From Amy's job hunt diary:

**Week 1:**
I absolutely hate interviewing for jobs, finding jobs, and even thinking about getting a new job. But my fresh, new layoff is overwhelming to me. Why did they do that? My track record for my employer was impeccable. I only had two sick days in the entire 14 years I worked there. Yet they cast me aside as if I were a box of overpriced paper clips. I'm still pissed off!

I don't know how they're going to get by without my work though. Nobody in Finance knows what I know about running things! And to dump me when the economy is like this? I am pretty specialized in my accounting work and not just any firm here in Oregon will want someone from my narrow niche of finance. I need to take a walk.

**Week 2:**

I have read several books and studied web sites on 'how to get a job in this market.' It all comes down to the activities of networking and "selling" me—stuff I HATE doing! I excel at Excel – not salesmanship. Hyping oneself is for infomercial guys like Billy Mays on TV. I hate self promotion.

My resume is finally done to my satisfaction. After four drafts which didn't feel right I finally went to a job coach. Like lawyers and CPAs he was overpriced, but he created a document I finally liked. Now, what to do with it?

**Week 3:**

At our church council meeting I told my dilemma to Les, the church council president. We work together closely because I head up the finance committee at church. Les is a VP of Sales for some local online advertising company that has grown pretty fast. He is a "honcho" over there, I guess. He is a bit on the arrogant side, but he offered to help me out so I agreed.

He immediately took me and my job search under his wing. I felt like one of his products he was selling. But that is OK because I need the help. I had spent the last two weeks frozen in what my job coach calls "A & A—Analysis and Anger." Les verified that and came up with new "A" words for me: "Attitude, Aptitude & Action."

He liked my resume and told me to be sure to customize it toward each company I wanted to send it to. For instance, if I were going to apply for an accounting position at a software company, I was to create bullet points which emphasized all my experience and accomplishments with various software packages. And then I should change the Key Word Summary on my resume to emphasize things relating to software. He said this is how I will differentiate myself from my competitors who don't customize their resumes for each job.

Les strongly encouraged me to build a profile on Linkedin.com. I told him I didn't want to become like my teen-aged nephew who filled his hours surfing nonsensical gibberish on FaceBook or MySpace. Les argued how having a profile on Linkedin.com was different from that and OK because it was a business network where I could build my "social capital."

I don't know what social capital is, but I used most of the content from my resume to build a profile on Linkedin. It was easy. I told Les though that I refuse to put my picture on my profile. My photo led to a lot of teasing in school. He said I am in control of what goes onto my profile.

**Week 4:**

I finished my profile on linked in but Les really jumped on me about my lack of activity. He was checking in on me via text messages one day and asking how many resumes I had sent out. He told me I needed to raise my number of prospecting contacts and rejections. It makes me feel like a pitch man but due to the economy he is right. He demanded I send out at least two resumes a day. When I replied with the fact that I was running out of places to send resumes, he sent me this bolded text message:

"THERE ARE 10,000 FIRMS IN OUR TOWN...MOST NEED ACCOUNTANTS!!"

That was clear and we later talked how I should apply for any job related to finance. If it were a bookkeeper or a CFO vacancy, I was encouraged to apply. He explained how someone might see something in my customized resume which may fit a need at their company. He said companies often have open positions which are not posted. He also said an internal person could get promoted into the position which was advertised therefore creating an opening which might fit me!

After our recent church council meeting Les told me we were going to move into a "Web 2.0 campaign for my job hunt. I guess that means we are going to use that Linkedin tool a lot more. He emailed me his list of "Ten LinkedIn Steps toward a Successful Job Hunt." I'm saving his list here (complete with my thoughts in italics):

1. Go to **www.linkedin.com** and create an account by filling in the fields under "Join Linkedin Today." It is free and easy. *I already did that but the phone hasn't rung!*

2. Then go to the **Advanced Search** link on the top of your profile page and type in name of a potential corporate employer which we'll call your Target Company. Research one company at a time. *I guess this is better than using the phone book.*

3. Study the names of the people listed under your Target Company. See if anyone listed there is someone you know from accounting or business associations you belong to, or from church, college, clubs, charities, relatives, hobbies, or even high school acquaintances. Write down their names even if you don't know them very well. *This seems silly!*

4. Click on those peoples' profiles and invite them to link in with you. Do this by clicking **"Add 'Les' to Your Network."** Be sure to personalize those invitations by finding any common ground you can find. And help them remember where they know you from or where they met you. Give them a reason for linking in with

you. Don't just use the generic messages that are the defaults under Linkedin invitations. *Makes sense.*

*When those people accept your invitation you will get an email telling you this. Thank them sincerely for linking with you. Also, scan their Connections for more people you might know. "NSN" -Never Stop Networking. *This sounds tiring.*

5. Don't look needy by asking your new Connections for job help right away. Compliment people on something they've posted on their profile or ask them a question about themselves. By asking people about themselves, you'll be asking them about their favorite subject! Chat a few times about generic topics and offer to be helpful to them. *What can I do for them? They already have a job!*

6. After some initial chat, it is OK to ask if they know of any accounting jobs, and if it feels right, perhaps ask for a connection inside their accounting department who might network with you. *This seems logical.*

7. When you get some positive nibbles, be prepared to use your "elevator speech." You remember an elevator speech is fifty words or less about why Your Unique Self can make a difference to their accounting department. Ask to meet them for a brainstorming lunch or a soda after work. *Again, this sounds tiring!.*

8. Repeat this process with ten other Target Companies.

   *It is just that easy, huh? This sounds time consuming. But I guess I have time now...*

9. There will be people listed at your Target Companies who you don't know but they are people who you do

want to have a dialog with. One way to invite them into your network is to pay for an upgrade to LinkedIn for a couple of months. That isn't that bad of an idea nor is it very expensive, but first, try the **LinkedIn Group Strategy:**

a. Many people on LinkedIn display the groups and associations they have joined through the site. Those interests are shown on the bottom of their profile under the topic "Groups and Associations." Their profile will also show "Groups you share with (name)," if there are any. It is your goal to share groups with strangers because that makes them approachable. Make notes on which groups they are part of.

b. Go to the **Groups** section of LinkedIn which is on the left side menu bar and click on it. Next, click on the **tab** called "**Groups Directory.**"

c. Then you'll see a pull-down menu on the right offering you some main categories. Clicking on any of them shows you thousands of groups you can join and/or use to further research your Target Companies and People. Let Your Fingers Do the Walking and be open to what you discover in this new treasure trove of categories and interests.

d. You should join several appropriate Groups—I think you can join up to 50 of them. Just click on the "Join Group" box which gives you a "settings" page. If you want to get group updates from the people IN those groups on a daily or weekly basis, check those boxes. If you want no updates, Uncheck the Digest Email box. Since you are looking for work, you likely want to see lots of updates from lots of people on a daily basis. This can get overwhelming to your email box if you join big groups, but you can always change this and cut back to have no updates later.

e. After you have selected your settings, click on the box again that says "Join Group." The next page will show you which groups you have joined or applied to join. The application goes automatically to the volunteer group leader but you can add a message to the group manager if you feel your case needs bolstering.

f. If you want to write a note to enhance your membership application, just be sincere and brief (something like, "I'd like to join your interesting group"). Most groups let anyone join so you'll likely be accepted. I join a lot of groups and have only been rejected once!

g. Once you belong to a Group "in common" with your Target People, you can invite members of that group into your network! Under the group heading you'll see a tab called "**Members.**" Click on it and there will be a list of everyone. Choose the one you want to engage by clicking on their name, then click on "**Add (name) to your network.**"

h. It will then ask you, "**How do you know (name)?**" Click on the **Group** you share with that Target Person and you will be able to send him or her an invitation to connect with you! You can even add a personalized note. Then use the strategies above in Steps 1 -6.

**10.** You can also use your own contacts to network with their contacts in Target Companies. Here is how you can get introduced through your present contacts:

> On the very bottom of a LinkedIn **Profile** look for **"Send a Message to (Name)."** There you click on **"get introduced through a connection."** That leads to a couple of self-explanatory boxes where you can address the person in your network AND the person they know who you want to be introduced to. This isn't as high a percentage hit ratio because some folks feel they are being "used," but it can often work OK. Remember, most people like to help!

ॐ

*Whew!* That was a lot of directions but after looking at the site and using my friend's road map, it is pretty easy. I thought someone had to be a techie to do these seemingly inside tricks but that's not true. The more I work with it the tool, the easier it all becomes. I don't need to fear it because there is nothing I can break.

ॐ

Les encouraged me after our last church council meeting to persist, persist, and persist because I only need one job. And Les gave me one more important reminder about Social Networking and Social Media:

*"Nobody ever hired a digit or a profile. Hiring is about relationships so use these tools to build deeper and more relationships."*

**Week 5:**

I kept doing most of what Les told me to do and two people have contacted me about interviews! One is a result of my profile on LinkedIn.com where I used a Group to invite a "stranger" into my network. She works at one of my Target Companies. I found her through the **Association for Latino Professionals in Finance and Accounting**. There are a lot of groups out there!

The other person met me through a friend of hers who saw my **"Network Updates: What Are You Working on Right Now?"** box. There I had listed "Searching for an employer who needs a stellar accountant." Her firm is interested in finding an Assistant Controller which is nowhere close to my level. But, they are small and I guess people wear a lot of hats at a place like that.

Les made me use that phrase in my update box. An introvert like me would have never used that phrase! But it worked!

ও

Before going on the interviews, Les and I had lunch. It had been many years since I had done any interviewing so I was glad he asked me to a long meal. I am lucky to have a guy like him on my side because he taught me the following "Three Big Things About Job Interviews:"

1.  The firm will want to know *if I have the skills to do the job*. They want to hear what ACTIONS I have taken to benefit former employers. They don't want to hear about my department or my division ("we")... they want to know what action and results I (as in, "me, myself, and I") have done which positively

helped the firm. Of course they want to know if I can collaborate, but they also want to know if I can get anything done by myself. I'm not supposed to say, 'We reduced the Accounts Payable cycle by three days.' Instead, I need to articulate what *I* did to make that happen.

2. Next, the potential employer wants to know *if I will fit in*. If a woman can do the job but doesn't fit into the firm's culture, style, philosophy, history, mission, or even their "vibe," then the deal is a non-starter.

    ◻ The potential employer wants to know if I am likeable and if I dress, look, and act like most of my potential peers and supervisors. They want to know if I can meld into the productivity of the team. If they suspect I'd *distract* from any of that, I won't get an offer. I never really thought about it, but I really did fit in well with my past employer.

3. Lastly, an interview is a way for an employer to see *if they want to afford me* as a candidate. Am I worth the pay I seek? They will want to compare me to the many other job seekers out there...

    ◻ Even though the Assistant Controller title is fancier than my last job, it might still have a lower pay range. I'll soon have an income of *zero* so I am very flexible and *will consider any reasonable offer!* Les says today companies are hunting for a deal and some will use the recession to offer lower salaries!

He gave me a homework assignment of creating three short sound bites (and memorizing them) about 'why these companies should hire me.' This is similar to his assignment of creating an Elevator Speech earlier. But he says I can never sound "canned."

I have a lot of questions written down before the interviews. My Target Company web sites offer lots of info and I think these firms will really be impressed when I ask them about stuff that is NOT on their web sites. I am pedantic!

The tool, **www.technorati.com** helps find lots of articles and info on lots of companies when I just type the Target Company name in their search box.

**Week 6:**

I got the job! The software company expects to bounce back strongly after the Recession of The Recession. Their hiring freeze now just means they can't add *new* headcount but they needed to replace my predecessor who is moving to Texas. I guess this is what Les meant by 'The Hidden Job Market.'

My salary is 12.3 % less than my old pay but Les reminded me how it took me 14 years to reach my *old* salary. The firm has promised me a six-month salary review. Cool!

Week 7

To celebrate my new job, Les asked me out to dinner! We have both been divorced for over a year. He taught me how to find and build relationships with people so I am going to use those strategies on him!

ह✿

Web sites which helped Amy can be found at **www.growmedia.com.**

# 3

# Keep Your Friends Close

## Mike Caters To Executive Tastes

Paul,

Here is the story of how I got my business started. You asked for a lot of historic detail so I gave you all the ingredients!

Mike

## Business Start-Up Journal

I have fifteen years of food service experience at age thirty because I started in food service when I was only fifteen years old. I worked up to thirty hours per week at fast food places during high school. I was never into sports, music or drama and my family liked it when I brought home a paycheck. Plus, the other co-workers at my fast-food employers became my social group. The three different franchised food operations I worked for while in high school were similar but different. I changed jobs for better pay and I learned more at each employer.

Upon my high school graduation, my manager wanted me to join his store as an Assistant Manager Trainee at a quick serve restaurant. I knew all the production sides of a restaurant but not the business side of the operation. Also, I had no human management experience other than training dozens of new workers. So, I signed on for that job to learn those things and also enrolled in the food services program at the local community college.

That education program taught me more about restaurant business and accounting functions. Also of interest to me was my favorite class about "food as an art form." I learned how food preparation and presentation can be a true "experience" for customers. I hadn't seen much of that at the burger and sandwich joints I had worked.

I earned a near-perfect GPA even though I was working full time. I was in my element and didn't really miss the partying and girl-chasing my peers seemed to have plenty of time for. Like always, my quick serve restaurant staff was my social outlet.

Upon graduation, I signed on as Assistant Manager with an upscale restaurant here in town. We offered "a unique dining experience" to our guests and that was a fun switch. It was a different life than the franchise world because an interesting local woman owned the restaurant. She was very concerned about her brand and the reputation of her establishment—things I had not seen before.

It was a very personable place and she knew many of her regular customers. I too got to know her and often picked her brain regarding the restaurant business. She liked that and gave me more and more responsibility over the next three years. But, her nephew was the main chef and there appeared to be nowhere to grow. Even though I was still young, I had the skills, I felt, to do more and be more. Hers was just a one-restaurant operation. The money was good and the environment great, but I felt dead-ended.

I ended up landing a position as the store manager of another upscale, casual dining café with an ethnic flavor. I joined them because they had thirty full-service restaurants across the southeast, assuring eventual upward mobility for me. This job was similar to my former employer—quality food, an upbeat staff, great money, and lots of hours. But this was my best employer yet because it is where I met Cindy.

She was a part-time waitress and college student. After we became "an item," I avoided any preferential treatment of her and kept things very professional at the restaurant. Only her close friends knew we were dating. We were married a year later.

At twenty-five, I became the youngest multi-store manager this restaurant group had ever had. I was managing store managers who were ten years senior to me. Most of my stores built profitability over time but the turnover of good managers was always a problem. It became even more of a problem when they had to report to a boss who was so much younger than they were. It seemed I was always doing new manager training.

After three years with the group and lots of travel to put out the fires caused by high turnover, I put my ears to the ground again. Through an online friend I learned about a job at a local country club. They needed a manager for their bar and restaurant operation. I had heard the pay at the club was outstanding. Plus, I felt I was ready to stop running around to several stores and just be at one location again. We had a two-year-old and another baby on the way. Cindy was more than ready to have me be in town more often.

The country club offered the best service, quality, and clientele. Not being overly sophisticated, I was surprised to land the job over other recruits who were more polished. I was told I had a reputation as a very hard worker who cared much about my customers. Guilty as charged!

I excelled at staff training, menu creativity, service improvement, and customer relations (it was cool how we would see the same customer members on such a repeat basis). It was as if I had matured at just the right time to thrive in the midst of this manicured clientele.

The club manager and board were very pleased by the way I eventually grew sales on several fronts and over-all profitability with regard to the food service function. I relaxed in my new found work home and kept getting to know the members who I saw frequently. I got to meet and get to know many well-connected and influential types since we were one of only four elite country clubs in the city.

After about a year of this work, I was button-holed by a club member who was the Chief Operating Officer for a large insurance company. He explained how his company had just lost their Director of Food Services and he was interested in having me run his employee cafeteria and executive dining room.

That kind of work didn't appeal to me since I was an "upscale" manager now. But, he eventually wore me down and lured me with the idea that I would have a "Director" title in a major corporation, more pay, and better fringe benefits for my growing family. He closed the deal when he explained there would be virtually NO weekend work and how I would run the whole show. After many years of working all hours, all the time, I finally gave in to his compelling pitch.

Corporate life was a different world for me. The executive and employee dining rooms were not profit centers for the corporation, so I had to fight for budget money to make improvements. Raising food prices was not an option either. I had no frame of reference for this new kind of accountability I had jumped into.

I made some cosmetic changes that were well received, but I was still a fish out of water. I enjoyed meeting and catering to the executives though—that felt like I was back at the club—except for the budget part. I got to know most of the "brass" well because they welcomed my creative "food events."

After I had been on the job for eighteen boring months, the insurance company had decided to bring in a national level food service/catering contractor that had promised them radical cost savings without a loss of quality. Perhaps their economies of scale could cut costs and maintain quality, but I didn't buy it.

They promised me a job, but at a reduced pay scale with poorer fringe benefits. I quit. Since age fifteen, I had worked long hours. I had never developed many hobbies outside of work other than video gaming, so I had done OK with saving my money. My father had been laid off seven times in his life so I guess I believed him when he beat it into my head to save my money and have a nice nest egg. Also, one whiz kid I had once hired at my second burger place had gone on to become some hero in the investment world. He had talked me into using him as a financial planner and he had focused on high tech stocks in the 1990s. The result of my savings and investments was that at age 30 I had a cash portfolio of $80,000. Money grows fast when you start young and don't spend much.

But I was also kind of naïve about life outside of the restaurant business. I wanted to take control of my life and became hell-bent on becoming my own man. I was an expert at creating dining experiences for upscale customers but had no idea as to how to find the $600,000 or more I would need to open my own fine restaurant.

So I needed another way to become my own man without that kind of investment. Cindy helped me realize that as a result of my club and executive dining room jobs, I had great community connections.

A friend of mine ran a great weddings and funerals catering business and he needed some event-oriented help. He offered to pay me some chump change to help him cover his busy season in June. I agreed since I had no other job and was intrigued by his business model.

I was like a sponge—I observed and absorbed everything about his operation. I realized that I was smart enough to run my own upscale catering business but that would mean many weeks of long hours and sporadic, even seasonal income. It didn't look like a family-friendly way to live and Cindy was adamant about staying home as a full time mom to the girls.

With Cindy's encouragement and after getting some advice from Service Corps of Retired Executives, I began launching my own niche-oriented catering business.

I asked several of my executive friends if they thought it was a good idea for me to try this. Since I was there asking them advice rather than trying to sell them something, they were very receptive. Everyone likes to be helpful if they have time and they already knew me so they made time. One heavy-set executive was a big customer in several ways back at the insurance company. He offered to finance me but I told him I was self-funded but that he could help by giving me referral business. I gave him some free cookie trays when I was in his neighborhood and he kept sending business my way. If I had engaged him as an investor, he would have eaten all my profits!

&

Cindy's PR background was also very helpful. She designed some cheap but elegant brochures and we had them created on the cheap at a local quick-copy shop. I would drop them off, attached to those cookie and treat trays to the offices of various executives I knew around town. This cost me gas money and some ingredient expense but proved to be a real boon to growing my business. Blueberry muffin arrangements seem to drive the most referral calls to me... food always opens doors!

Cindy is also a whiz on Internet visibility. She finds blogs in the local print media that discuss food and hospitality. and she always manages to slip a subtle plug in for our business. She also networks via something called www.LinkedIn.com but I am too busy making meatballs to know how that keeps getting us inquiries about our upscale services.

One marketing trick I used was to stop at a company's offices and say something like "Steve the CEO needs this cookie tray before his 3:00 tee time." I often knew Steve did have a three o'clock tee time and gatekeepers at the front desk therefore sensed my confidence and got my dessert bribes right up to him. Of course I included my big business card which includes my photo to refresh their memory.

People ask me where I came up with the cash to host my own food preparation facility. We are way beyond working out of my home kitchen. What I did was to subcontract with my friend who caters weddings. Together we rent time and space at a commercial bakery which produces food only during certain hours of the day. Therefore they enjoy the rent money my friend and I pay in order to use their commercial equipment and walk in coolers after their working hours. They are a bakery products firm so they are done with their own space by 2:00 in the afternoon.

In the early days, I rented my serving equipment "as needed" but now I am well on my way to acquiring all that I need. My wedding business friend says we should open our own preparation/storage facility, but I remember too well the narrow profit margins in my early days of food. Nothing is a sure bet and you have to keep your overhead costs lean and mean. I will rent that prep facility on the cheap as long as I can. There is no upside to having an expensive facility of my own, especially since I have backup facilities all lined up.

Cindy's mom watches the kids when my wife wants to help with preparation, serving, and on-site customer relations. The clients just love her and I do too! Her nieces, nephews, and cousins (she has a HUGE family) help serve our larger corporate gigs. They are all nice teenagers who do great with minimal training.

I am not surprised at the robust interest in my services even in this tough economy. Executives have money to spend and will actually spend it on the things they want. And they always want things done my way—first class.

By using me as a vendor who works outside of their normal in-house, executive food budget, they can turn me loose at high-level client entertainment events. We have had some really cool food events for their high-level sales prospects and executive meetings. Those kinds of gigs are very profitable!

In summary, my job transitions led to the destination I am now at and which I enjoy greatly. People need to build on their strengths, cultivate their current relationships and use their imaginations. That is the perfect recipe for success!

Bon` Appetite!

❧

For web sites which were helpful to Mike,
please see **www.growmedia.com**.

# 4

# Discover Your Hidden Assets

## Insurance Manager Renee Discovers a New Path

*Paul,*

*As promised, I am finally getting a summary of my journal to you. I struggled after the layoff, but it all came together. Here's my story:*

I enjoyed almost every moment of my career in the insurance industry. My friends think I am odd for saying that—especially after twenty-four years in the field. My first job out of college was as an Assistant Claims Auditor Trainee. From "Day One," I liked the feeling of helping customers at our regional processing center.

One thing I *didn't* feel good about though, was my recent lay-off. Ninety other employees were cut the same day I got the axe. I felt bad for them too, but I couldn't get over the fact that my employer actually cut ME! How would they ever get along without me? You'd think they would appreciate what I have done for them... After hundreds of policy/procedure reviews, budget meetings, peer training sessions, morale and team building activities, and business process improvement projects, I've saved that company fifty times my salary!

And I did that happily because I am a subject-matter expert. Few people in the company know what I know and can do what I do. I learned a TON over all those years there and was the best they had, or will ever have, at what I did. My most recent boss there was probably in diapers when I started working for the company, and he often took credit for my work! Looking back on things I realize it isn't enough just to do a good job and assume that everyone who matters notices that.

I loved my staff there. My whole team of 12 stood by me when the axe fell. A couple even threatened to quit if I was let go! My past morale building efforts apparently paid off. We were more than a bunch of co-workers. We were almost like family.

When they wanted to rise up in arms when they heard about my layoff, I reminded them not to get stupid because our small city had few jobs that paid what they earned. They had to keep their heads and I told them *my* departure might make their job security a little better.

❧

Now what? There were few jobs in town that paid what I had to earn. And insurance was all I had ever done and all I know. My time at the company had been good to me financially. Even small annual percentage raises added up nicely when there were twenty-four of them! I made more than my husband Bill, and his income alone couldn't cover our family's needs. People told me to go into selling the health insurance that I processed for all those years, but I knew that I wouldn't be a fit for that line of work.

I had few interviews in our Midwestern city, population 45,000. We just don't have the same job market that Minneapolis or Des Moines does. Finding a well-paying job was tough since my whole career to date had been spent in that Regional Processing Office. There were few other big companies in town. We only had branch offices and franchises for the most part except for the combine plant which always seems to be laying off people too.

There was a possibility at the biggest bank in town. It was a major employer and had good benefits. Their pay range was even in the ballpark of what I used to make. But, they eventually hired another person. She was about my age but she had actually worked in a bank before so that must have been the reason. I suppose the fact that she is three or four dress sizes smaller than me made a difference too. I guess those things matter to a bank.

I had to learn to not take rejection personally. This came through a couple of counseling sessions with our pastor. He was wise and calming when I gushed about my lack of marketability in our city. He helped me to finally realize that I am not a bad person just because my job market niche stinks.

While searching for the "hidden job market," I read a book which said the phrase simply means "word of mouth" hiring. I hadn't gotten anywhere with online job boards. My lame resume was posted on three national resume banks but I never got a call from any of that. I did get a few emails encouraging me to stuff envelopes and other home-based or Internet-related millionaire schemes which required a "small" fee to get started. So, I figured all I could do was ramp up that word of mouth thing. I figured I'd be good at that because I have a big mouth!

I made a list of everyone I knew within fifty miles. I listed where they worked and what they did. Via phone, email, Twitters, and in person I asked everyone listed about possible jobs at their employers. I had found about 40% of these friends, relatives, church members and acquaintances on **www.linkedin.com, www.Facebook.com** and even Twitter. com. It took a lot of time to research and dig all that out and to create all those connections, but time was what I had. I was treating my job search like a full-time job because my severance pay was half gone after three months.

Many who heard about my layoff were happy to help me brainstorm. People really are willing to help if you ask nicely—even people who you don't know very well. I learned that one "trick" is to ask acquaintances for help. They are often willing to help you but resistant to being "sold" on helping you. They often ignore you if you are too demanding or simply expect them to take their valuable time to help you.

My plan uncovered six leads, two interviews, and one offer I turned down due to the low salary. But this flurry of activity actually led to a job offer, and that improved my morale. I was thinking I maybe should have taken the job which was offered to me, but it was an office manager in a one-horse office and the owner of the service business was kind of creepy. I wasn't that desperate yet. I was doing what my job coach in that book told me to do: "Increase your number of rejections."

In my purse, I always carried three, colored CDs each burned with a different version of my resume. I gave away a total of five CDs during various family, social, church, and business-related events. Their bulky and colorful presence reminded me to be networking constantly.

I also had simple business cards printed up with my name, phone numbers, email address, and a "branding sentence" which had my name and read:

*"Seek to utilize seasoned administrative, managerial or hands-on skills to improve your organization's operational efficiency."*

A couple of people I gave those to asked if I was an independent consultant. I told them I was only seeking a full time job. If I had been open to temporary work, those little cards would have landed me two or three short-term gigs, I'm sure. But, I was still holding out for a full time, career-type of position.

❧

Those CDs in my purse reminded me of my job hunt during a regular office visit with Dr. Smith. She and I were discussing my ongoing medication so I grabbed my prescription bottle from my purse and noticed the resume disks again. When she asked about my stress, it was a golden opportunity to tell her about my search and availability. She was on my "contacts" list but not on the social networking sites, so I hadn't approached her.

We chatted how my unemployment could well be contributing to my higher blood pressure. After I gave her a fifteen second "elevator speech" of my capabilities, she thought for a moment and mentioned how she had an idea for me. She asked me to call her in a week.

Dr. Smith is a shareholder at her large medical practice.

She had just been to the practice's business meeting where it was announced their reimbursement administrator had resigned. I learned this after my follow up call to her a week after our appointment.

With Dr. Smith as my 'foot in the door,' I earned an interview for the position. It was not a perfect fit for me as it was a side of the insurance business I had not worked on. But it *was* about insurance. I sold the interview panel on how I could easily learn the reimbursement and provider-relations part due to my 'many years in the industry.'

I heard through one of my social groups of another woman who had interviewed for that job. I was very stressed out about that because I knew of her. She used to work at the hospital. I couldn't stand waiting so I scheduled a follow-up medical appointment with Dr. Smith for my blood pressure!

She was surprised to see me just two weeks after our earlier appointment and I told her I was concerned about my blood pressure because of the interview process. She laughingly explained how the business manager had been traveling and nothing much was being done on the vacancy in his absence. Dr. Smith also told me in a quiet tone how the other job candidate was more qualified than me but the committee like my personality better!

"Employers always try to hire the most likeable person," she mentioned with a smile and a wink. My blood pressure went down on the spot!

The practice's business manager came back from his ski vacation and offered me the job at money close to what I used to make. I love working in this environment in a job I never even would have thought of. I am glad I carried my job hunt reminders with me everywhere!

This is a smaller, friendlier employment setting. I like

being part of helping our group's patients with complicated and important paperwork. Dr. Smith certainly helped me cure my career ailments!

ॐ

See **www.growmedia.com** for websites which were helpful to Renee.

# 5

# Look For Local Opportunities

## Controller Kevin Coddles Start-Ups

My best friend Kevin returned to our hometown after living and working in Dallas for years. Career-wise, he was a medium fish in a bigger sea down there in the big city. He had earned a Vice President/Controller job with a mid range high-tech firm. He worked very hard in that job—I know because it would take him weeks to answer emails from me. Even emails about fishing! He moaned now and then about the long hours, lack of structure, and the shifting politics at his fast growth company. But, it was an exciting ride and he was smart enough to enjoy the experience and its many perks.

After some struggles were announced, his employer announced a layoff of 2,000 workers, occurring over a twelve month period of time. Kevin was part of the cuts and he'd seen it coming being a numbers guy and all. I just don't think he ever thought it would actually affect him.

That kind of layoff is sure different than the way things

work around here. In our town of 40,000, people don't do things like that. Everything is fairly stable and steady and nothing much changes other than how the big city keeps creeping closer and closer to us. It was just announced a "technology park" would be built on the edge of town in order to encourage companies to consider relocating here.

When Kevin asked me if I knew of any jobs around here, I smiled because I thought he had outgrown us. Unemployment affects ones' overall attitude, I guess. He convinced me that he wanted to move back home and slow down a bit. I was glad because that could mean I get my old high school fishing buddy back!

A guy I knew through the Lions Club was retiring from his job at the city's biggest manufacturing plant. The job wasn't a high profile one like Kevin had, but our cost of living is low and our lifestyle is good. Kevin had told me he could get by on less money since his kids had their own homes now and his wife was eager to downsize their home in the Dallas suburbs. Again, his pending unemployment apparently forced openness to life modifications sooner than planned.

He was always conservative with his money so I figured his nice nest egg would allow him to afford the job here. I'm sure it would only pay half of what he used to make, if that much!

He got the job here because he convinced the facility's manger that he wanted to come home, slow down, and help out a smaller company. He relocated back here in time for our thirtieth high school reunion. His nice house down near Dallas sold quickly despite the bad economy.

Kevin and his wife found a cozy ranch up here for about half the price of their old place. It needed some work but Kevin was always pretty handy and seemed to like the idea of fixing up a place. He settled into a routine of working in an "underemployed" manner at our plant by day, and doing home repairs in the evenings. On weekends we fished a lot! He contributed a lot to that plant for over two years. His superior understanding of business, finance, technology, and modern processes and procedures saved them significant money and he told me he really enhanced their profitability. He was a hero to all who understood his work. He loved the place, including his really short workweek of only 40 hours per week.

❧

In March, of this year, the corporate office sold the plant and the new buyer planned to move its function to Mexico. There was a loud outcry in the community since about 150 jobs would be lost. Kevin was dismayed since he felt "settled" until the news broke. So, here he was in our small city and unemployed again. He wanted an income so he could protect his nest eggs for retirement. But here he was, in a town which was trying hard to recruit new jobs and employers but struggling to do so.

For weeks he tried to land a job in his area of finance. The economy was tight, jobs were sparse, and nobody wanted to hire a high-paid, "fifty-ish" guy from a "big shot" Dallas firm. The expression, "You can't come home again" must have seemed true to Kevin. There were just very few prospects in a town our size.

While networking with people, Kevin began to meet a few professionals who were in various phases of doing start-up ventures. He connected with them via **www.linkedin.com** where they have blogs and special interest groups and more about this kind of thing, I am told. The economy had just tanked but there were still some good product and service ideas out there. Some of those new ventures still had angel investment money behind them. The six different company founders who he was visiting with, had, according to Kevin, "no clue of what they were doing when it came to financing and operating a start-up venture and maintaining cash flow." He had seen all of this before in Dallas.

Kevin had structured various independent contractor and consultant deals many times for his Dallas employer. He realized these maverick start-ups *needed* to do some of that to support their growth. In a blinding flash of the obvious, he realized his expertise could really help.

None of the smaller or emerging firms could afford him on a full-time basis however. And some of them had their hands tied pretty tightly due to the financial controls their investor groups had put on them. Yet, many of them really needed some daily or weekly governance from an accounting standpoint.

Kevin was not a self promoter. He did set up a profile on www.linkedin.com, but his personal introductions via his attendance of service club meetings helped to open the most doors. His local chamber of commerce, though small, did a good job of setting up networking meetings. At these types of events Kevin was generally introduced to one or two new entrepreneurial leaders in the community. And he always had his nondescript business card at the ready. After two months he found four firms that were open to possibly "renting" his expertise on a part-time basis. His "name-brand" technology company experience really gave him credibility, he later said.

My fishing buddy structured varying deals with these firms. He had ongoing retainers and numerous short-term gigs. Kevin billed by the hour, or project, or monthly basis based on the needs of his clients. He priced himself in a similar range to the local CPAs and managed to stay busy, on and off, for 20 to 30 hours a week. He made clear that he was going to stay focused on corporate accounting and not personal income tax work.

Word of Kevin's services spread from person to person. His track record as a former financial exec from a big brand name firm helped him to reach a personal "tipping point." He fine-tuned his profile on the social media network and watched the number of visitors to his profile grow. He started inviting many people from the county and this increased his "traffic" there too. He even showed me how he used the WordPress.com tool on LinkedIn to dabble with blogging.

That wasn't his thing though—I think it seemed too extroverted for him. He found a way to use that tool without having to say too much though. He told me one Saturday at the fishing hole how he'd just toss a brief, provocative questions onto his blog. Then, the people who followed his blog would do all the "talking" and he'd just serve as an aloof moderator and facilitator. He used the tool www.technorati.com to help him sort out trending content and to look smart and help feed his blog.

When I said that all sounded complicated he told me he simply clicked on "Applications" on the left side of the LinkedIn.com home page. There was the icon for WordPress. com and he simply followed a couple of clicks there to be in the blogging business.

"And," he said, "I don't have to spend much time on my blog at all because I just facilitate the conversation of others and I do it every Friday afternoon right after lunch. That way people know when to check it." As usual, Kevin is the picture of efficiency!

His last way to sell for a guy who hates to sell was to form a group on LinkedIn.com which was an entrepreneur club for start-ups in our county. It is just called our county's entrepreneur club and it is a way for young firms to come together and collaborate. It is a breeding ground, I hear for *new* firms within fifty miles of our town. They don't meet physically but Kevin gets lots of leads from this via the participants' general questions on the group forum. And members all stumble upon that forum themselves.

Kevin did nothing but start the group by clicking on "Groups" on the left side tool bar on his profile page. He showed me how to click there and then click on "Create a Group" which gives you all sorts of options about how you want your group to run and look. It is free, easy and the members find Kevin's group and apply to him to join. He does *nothing* to recruit members! He showed me the group is already up to 47 members. I am going to form one for fishing!

➰

Kevin recently moved out of his home-based office into a small space just off Main Street. He laughed when he told me that one *year's* rent on this office was less than one *month's* rent for a similar space in Dallas. He said he felt more professional by having his own place where he could more easily meet clients. He said they respected him more that way too.

His membership in Optimists, Kiwanis, Rotary, and Lions, SCORE and Toastmasters have helped him be the salesman he isn't.

In less than a year, Kevin was turning away business. He avoided hiring employees other than a part-time assistant. People encouraged him to expand but he loved finally being in control of his hours, earnings, and destiny.

It is good to finally be able to go fishing again with my friend!

⁂

To see web sites which were helpful to Kevin, please go to www.growmedia.com.

# 6

# Discover Your Natural Market

## VP Val Does Vertical Vendor Relations

After 8 years, Val was laid off from her VP of Information Technology position at a large hospitality services company. The slower economy was blamed, but Val suspected possible gender issues too. *A few of the male C-levels don't like a woman in this job,* she mused to herself, and they finally used the economy as a way to get me out. The CEO who had promoted her to the position had retired 3 years prior.

Val had worked in computer-related positions in her hometown for the past twenty-one years, and she earned her BS and MBA at a local university. She was very well connected due to high involvement with a dozen different civic, charitable, and industry associations and organizations. At a recent technical conference, she realized how her local IT community felt like a big, small town.

Her severance package included a year of her annual salary plus paid health insurance for that long. Her payout was better than the 30 others who were also laid off the same day as she got cut. Her officer status helped fatten up her departure allowance.

That payout, her former six-figure salary, plus her careful investments over the past years allowed Val to not need an income for about two years if she didn't want to. But she and her husband, who had a good job, wanted to add to, not reduce their attractive nest egg. And the economy had shrunk their aggressive investments by nearly 40% so she was motivated to keep earning. Plus, she liked the stimulation of work and wanted to get back to that after taking three months off following her separation. She had done all the painting and redecorating she wanted to do in their nice house in their southwestern city of 300,000 people.

Finding and landing a job similar to her old one in her smaller city proved to be a challenge, but nobody was better connected than Val. She had dozens of lunch and cocktail meetings with friends and folks in senior roles in companies all around town. The recession had made everyone who had a job hunker down and keep their jobs so few positions were open, especially at the senior level of IT management. And there were not many large IT shops left. Some of the firms had outsourced their work to India, Brazil, Ireland or the Philippines. It seemed staffs and managerial responsibilities were shrinking rather than growing like they did in the roaring 1990s when Val had made her best career moves.

A trend Val noticed during her job hunt was how companies were reducing their IT vendor lists due to the high number of product and service providers who were constantly knocking on their doors. They were streamlining their negotiation efforts and reducing the number of suppliers. In the Internet age, it had become too easy for vendors from anywhere to find and knock on the doors at potential client companies. The volume of contracts and sales calls had become overwhelming to the buyers. Culling the vendor herd seemed to become a new mantra in Val's city.

Disparate vendors who provided everything from raised floors, computer cables, computer hardware, software, operating systems, storage, staffing services for temporary and permanent talent, wireless and wired networks, telecommunications services, IT training, offshore services, co-located disaster recovery services, data security services, etc. were all clamoring harder and harder than ever for a piece of the client pie.

Val knew IT leaders spent too much time screening, and responding to these many products and services companies in order to procure the things they needed to run their departments. Purchasing departments were too often circumvented during the vendor process because of their lack of familiarity with specific IT needs and the proprietary language and culture of technology.

A well-placed friend at Val's former employer told her about a recent capital equipment purchase. Val was surprised to hear the large price difference between that purchase and a friend's purchase of a very similar product.

Also, Val had heard from her insider friends how the new male CIO at her former employer was already freezing up due to the deluge of vendors pouncing on him like "a new piece of meat," He even called Val for advice on a couple of enterprise-level RFPs she was studying before she left. This all got Val to thinking about what she knew about the vendor community.

&

A job coach who had been provided to Val upon her layoff had put her through an exercise where she made a long list of her personal and professional assets. Even seemingly minor or inane assets were to be included–things like 'a pleasant personality.' On that list, she'd listed her vendor management skills and widespread IT community relationships. She hadn't given those attributes much thought.

Val had rampant industry involvement, local undergraduate and graduate college connections, high visibility at high-profile former employers, deep community and charitable involvement, and a stellar group of connections on the **www.linkedin.com** network. She built her LinkedIn profile to nearly 300 people she knew in and outside of her IT industry.

Her connections literally worked at all the significant employers in and around her city. Val targeted two dozen of her town's leading companies and listed all of her key connections at those firms who had decision-making authority over IT department budgets and expenses.

Next, she perfected her "Elevator Speech" which was nearly a minute long and then her "twitterVator speech" which was a twenty-word pitch about her skills. *People don't have much more time than that for a pitch*, she knew. A friend at an outside-the-box PR firm helped cull down Val's storied career into this strategic sound bite and Val was ready to make her pitch.

Some of her Master Mind Support Group suggested Val was "above" having to pitch herself as a consultant. She disagreed, knowing she'd not gotten where she had without quietly stating her own case for years.

She was on her way to offering to reduce or remove the burdens of vendor management for her potential new clients.

She formed a Limited Liability Corporation with $50 and a form at her state's Secretary of State's Office. Then she lined up Errors and Omissions insurance through an insurance agent she knew from her health club. And she never stopped tweaking her online social/business networking profiles and constantly invited more connections.

᠀

A few shops in town had a dedicated IT purchaser or asset manager or a person in HR who handled the staffing procurement side. But most didn't have those functions centralized or strategically orchestrated. Because of her elite credentials and warm introductions into them, several companies welcomed her in so they could gain an outside, neutral third-party, evaluation of their major technology bids.

Director-level and above executives typically knew or had heard of Val, or were comfortable with her high level of skill and reputation. They knew she'd "been there, done that" from their side of the desk. Val's concept of saving her clients the time and hassle of dealing with the products and service community had appeal. They seemed open to letting her provide them with efficient, astute, and *neutral* recommendations. "Hundreds of man-hours saved" Val often punned—*by a woman.*

After becoming engaged by a company, she did a great job of running interference with people who were selling enterprise-level products or services. Val's early clients were able to defer dozens of their vendor voicemails, emails and texts to Val, if and when they were in the market for a product upgrade or a services project.

She'd gather her clients' requirements and often fine-tune

what they *thought* they needed. Then she did the initial vendor research and collected the best set of bids, quotes, and prices. Her clients' final decisions usually followed most parts of her recommendations. And her reputation spread. Some clients allowed her to use her small successes with them on her social media sites.

Some of Val's clients paid by the hour, some paid her for the procurement "project" or a flat consulting fee, and others paid her a percentage of the perceived savings that she had driven out of the bids and procurement efforts.

Her assignments typically only lasted one to three months to finish her part of the process. Usually, she would initially assess the client needs at the client company's location. That lasted for 1 to 3 weeks, depending upon the scope of the procurement.

Thereafter, Val would work out of her state-of-the-art home office or meet over lunch with various vendors to collect, cull, and cleanse her research. It was a case study in juggling dozens of phone calls, meetings, and text messages each day and she loved the action. She always held back at least 10% of her time to focus on her procurement of her next gig.

Some of Val's consulting had significant positive impact for her clients and therefore significant positive impact for her financially. Other gigs were small or fleeting and some potential assignments were frozen in the tough economy. But she did Profit From the Recession since she was saving her clients significant money on purchases they had to make anyway.

Val became a master at pushing out several, informative and strategic messages a week to the hundreds of people in her social and business networks on LinkedIn and Twitter.

Different messages went to different groups since she had three distinct profiles on Twitter. Soon she had dozens of people following her Tweets (short, public, news updates) on Twitter.

That kind of action kept her face and name in front of many. Therefore she was never too far away from the hot procurement news on the street. These connections also ensured a network of helpful friends and experts who were quick to give her counsel in areas where she needed support.

Val ended up staying as busy as she wanted to be. She had some engagements which paid very, very well but other times she had no assignments at all. It averaged out to be about what her former earnings were, except now her income came in bursts instead of a steady paycheck. But, she felt much more self actualized and in control of her life and schedule. She also now had time for her passion of hot air ballooning.

Val loved the recognition of being an "on-demand" and an "in-demand" consultant. Now the only person she had to manage was her husband.

She is laid off and loving it and sometimes wishes she would have started her Vendor Relations consulting practice sooner.

ॐ

For resources which were helpful to Val,
please see **www.growmedia.com**.

# 7

# Follow the Path of
# Least Resistance

## President Perry Sells Insider Knowledge

Fred,

After our chat at our 40th high school reunion, I realized you were struggling with some early retirement issues. Perhaps my story will be helpful to you to you as you make your final decisions about the next steps in your life. This is a long email, but I hope you'll benefit from hearing my whole story:

I'd been President at my former employer for twelve years. The board originally brought me in to repair their many production, distribution, and sales problems. I knew accepting that job was risky, but after a lot of work we became profitable. The company made and distributed durable medical products and I had worked before as a VP for one of their larger competitors.

It was a lot of work. Some painful human resource actions helped clean up some old messes there. They had gotten sloppy and had lots of dead wood around. Changing many business processes and procedures, downsizing those 100 people (I hated doing that), outsourcing some of our operations, and upgrading almost half of our equipment were all the keys to our march toward profitability. I worked much longer than I wanted, and spent way too much time on the road, becoming an absentee father. Mary was a stay-at home mom and devoted herself to the kids but I still wished I hadn't missed so many soccer games and school plays.

After about four years of steady improvement, the company turned the corner and started earning a profit. The market and the economy were helpful to me on this but without the long hours and changes I put in we would have never even been around to exist and enjoy the good times. I was a hero in the eyes of our board. Profits and operations were chugging along smoothly and I got bored.

Since I had put so much of myself into this company for so many years, I couldn't see myself moving over to go to work for a competitor, even though I had a handful of head-hunter calls to do so. Instead, I figured I would retire early and become "Super Grandpa, the Wannabe Golf Pro."

The crisis days appeared to be behind the firm and the board apparently felt they could pay a younger president less money to keep things "status quo." They were probably right. A very satisfactory early retirement compensation plan was offered to me on my 60th birthday.

પ

After settling in as an early retiree, we saw more of the grandkids. Those young kids have full schedules and we attended some of their events since all of their parents live within an hour of us in our Atlanta suburb. We also had many visits from them on the weekends. There were a lot of comings and goings and our swimming pool was popular. The bottom line is that they didn't have the kind of time that I did, so I sometimes felt a little shortchanged. But, at least I got to see them more often than most of my peers got to see their grandkids.

After six months of golfing and two nice trips with Mary, I started to get a bit bored. On those international trips I met at least ten other tourists who asked in one form or another "What kind of work do you do?" and I would tell them I was retired. They'd nearly always look at me funny and some would even say that I was too young-looking to be retired. And I started to think they were right!

Being a "Type A" personality, I began looking for new worlds to conquer. Numerous charitable causes wanted to soak up my time and I did join a few boards and some of their committees. That was all well and good but I belonged in their executive offices, not serving soup and sandwiches. It is not that I am above any kind of work or any kind of people. It was just that I couldn't stop thinking about dozens of operational improvements I could make to these charities and I was powerless to make those changes.

I learned from the friends I left behind at our firm that one of my former employer's divisions was struggling in this economy. Some offshore issues had stopped working and the VP of that group was in over his head. Being very familiar with these problems and their solutions, I approached the new president with an idea. He and I had gotten to know each other during his transition into the job.

The new man had not been through several scenarios in his youngish career and he was very open to my input and ideas. At first he wanted me to keep our informal mentoring out of public view. He reminded me of my oldest son, and it made me feel useful to have someone who wanted to hear my old war stories. I made sure he, and eventually the board all knew my motives were *not* to make a roaring comeback.

"I just want to keep a finger in the business world," I told them all. "I'm not as good a golfer as I thought and the Senior PGA roster seems to be full up." That summary defused a lot of peoples' concern about why I was back with my hat in my hands to an employer which I appeared too glad to leave less than a year prior. I assured everyone that I would never assume a full time role and would prefer to only work six to nine months out of the year.

The contract I eventually offered the new president included those stipulations and made it clear I was only there to help. I insisted I never be allowed to set foot in the corporate office unless needed there for some critical issue. I also mandated I be based out of my home office and not work at the corporate office. I stated a strong preference of no more than four days per month of business travel—I need to keep working on my golf game you know! The agreement also clearly stated I was not to ever be considered for any full time position with the company.

This set of rules set the board at ease. We all tried it and the arrangement worked out nicely. They didn't need to train me on anything and the folks in the field realized that the old man from the corner office actually did know a thing or two! Actually, working out in the field as a roving consultant taught me more than I would care to admit. It is amazing how isolated one gets working in the corporate office even though I tried to "Manage by Walking Around."

After five months of this arrangement, we are spending the perfect amount of time with the grandkids. My daughter and her husband got to go on a couple of their own short trips while we watched the kids for nearly a week. I was ready for my own out of town business travel assignment after five nights of watching a six year old and a four year old. That daycare stuff is harder than running a company!

కి

The bottom line Fred is I recommend semi-retirement over real retirement. And, your *former employers* are the best companies to appreciate a senior fellow like you. Just because we enter our sixties doesn't mean we should be put out to pasture! Those new punks at Corporate have learned new things from me even though they'll never admit it. And, I have learned a lot too. It is very stimulating to be back out in the field offices amongst the troops where I haven't worked in 15 years.

And, it is really great when I don't have all the responsibility anymore. That means I can cut out on a fairly short notice to take a nap or torture a few golf balls. It is a nice blend.

I don't make near the money I used to make but that's OK because the house is paid for, the kids are educated, I don't like exotic travel, and Mary doesn't have too many expensive habits or hobbies. She is getting to be a more interesting golf partner plus we serve on a couple of charitable boards together.

So dust off your sales skills and pitch one of your recent employers on being a part time, inside consultant. Be sure to be non-threatening and tell them how you can save them big bucks compared to those $400 an hour types with all the brand names. You'll probably get some cheap or free travel perks out of the deal, and work in some visits to your grandkids. It works for me!

I'll also clue you in on this new thing they all call "social networking." It is the Rolodex of the 2000's and it is called LinkedIn.com. I'll write you out a recommendation on it when you get registered on this free service. I'll make you sound like the perfect insider...

I wish you luck. Let me know if I can do anything else to help.

Best wishes,
Perry

&

For web sites which were helpful to Perry, see **www.growmedia.com**.

# 8

## Explore New Ways to Serve

### Severed Software Executive Sells Seminars to Women

After a technical and sales career, Sandy started her own software company eight years ago. She grew it to twenty-four employees and was mildly successful at serving her small financial services niche with her product. She had been working in her industry niche for over twenty years. When she realized her market was changing and consolidations and new technology were going to negatively impact all she had done, she planned a new strategic direction.

But her angel investors and advisory board disagreed with her vision. Along the way, a few of her early employees sold their shares to the firm's financial backers and Sandy was suddenly a minority shareholder. After one more year of conflict and a slowdown of sales, Sandy conceded and agreed to be bought out.

The $2 million sales price was fair, based on the firm's

sales volume, recent cash flow, and industry potential. She was just pleased to be out of the company that had turned on her after she literally dedicated her whole life to it for so long.

To get her payout though, she had to sign a three-year, non-compete agreement that prevented her from working in the software niche she knew best. *No problem*, she thought... *I never want to be around this cutthroat, good-old boy industry again!*

After the deal was done, Sandy took a long Caribbean vacation and worked to unwind the knots caused from two decades of stress. She hadn't always been able to make payroll or get or keep new customers so the work had been hard on her.

ॐ

Upon her return, Sandy slowly began researching her next conquest. She struggled to find an industry, business, or niche that felt right. *I have been in the banking software niche since I got out of college...I don't know anything else!*

Sandy golfed and lunched once a week at the country club where she belonged. She never felt overly comfortable there due to a lack of other senior-level professional women members.

One day, she overheard a male member talking about her after he thought she'd left the room. The blowhard stated loudly, after several drinks, how Sandy's success was just due to "lucky timing." She almost came around from behind him and shouted *Pardon me? I slaved for twenty three years to become an overnight success!* But she restrained herself.

The big talker was the son of the founder of a successful business which was handed down to the rude club member. Sandy detested this kind of guy who she referred mockingly to as a "self made millionaire—the kind who takes a twenty-million dollar company and turns it into a twenty-ONE million dollar company."

She knew firsthand what was involved in starting a business and building it from scratch. She knew firsthand how it felt to have control wrested away. She knew firsthand the challenges of being a female business owner. She should have thanked the man because his comments subconsciously fueled her next occupational steps.

Sandy dedicated $200,000 of her cash to create an enterprise that empowers women to start, grow, and perhaps sell their own successful businesses. There were several government programs and non-profit associations with a similar focus, but few were actually run by people with Sandy's level of front-line business experience. Some of these "women's programs" were headed up by men!

She networked and researched extensively through every kind of local chamber of commerce function and association and church she could find. She created several Special Interest Groups and Affiliate Entrepreneurial Groups on social network pages at no cost since those sites like to see people build groups and the traffic that follows.

Sandy's background was mostly in sales and operations. Despite the fact that she built a software product company, she had always relied on her lead technical employees to handle that side of the house. This time she needed a go-to tech person to help create and manage her endeavor's web site. She engaged the son of a cousin who was an IT major at a local university famed for its web development programs. She paid him a nice hourly rate as an independent contractor who would get a 1099 tax form from her company at the end of the year. Sandy's virtual presence was supported by this part-time employee who worked from his home. He used this part-time work as the core for several of his college projects.

Sandy had uncovered a hidden need for business start-up advice for women. Many women wanted to take control of their occupational lives either full time or part time but too few knew how to take the next steps, or were too afraid to do so.

Over the course of the next six months, Sandy developed a plan to be a "for profit" consultant and broker to women who needed her information, inspiration, introductions, and mentoring services in their business start-ups. Few women were capitalized well enough to start ambitious endeavors so Sandy worked to help them to find money and investors if appropriate to their business plans. She steered those who needed financing toward the Small Business Administration's entrepreneurial division and occasionally to some angel investor groups she knew of. She chose not to be an investor in any of her clients.

Most of the time, Sandy would only take a deferred fee for her services. She told some clients to "Pay me when you become profitable," or, "Pay me with tiny pieces of owner-ship or stock for now." This drove many new clients her way since she was reputed as someone who was not a cash drain on young start-ups.

Sandy held low-cost, regional seminars promoting female entrepreneurship. Sometimes she secured vendor/sponsor companies that offered services which might be needed by the start-ups, such as Paychex or similar business support services. Those firms would invite their own prospects to Sandy's seminars in order to build positive traffic for all the non-competing firms present.

County and state economic development offices would

support Sandy too. Her content was similar to what they were always preaching but they recognized Sandy's 'real life' story as compelling.

On her seminar circuit, Sandy always brought and left media units of booklets, CDs, small capacity memory sticks with content and templates on them, and give-away items which reminded people about her Podcasts and download-able audible content. She had developed these materials with the help of a ghost writer over the first year in her new business. She was also toying with the concept of posting a funny or satirical video on YouTube.com in order to drive viral traffic where people would refer their friends to see the content. She realized this kind of presentation had its reputation risks but she wanted to consider all possible social media into her mix.

The most enjoyable outcome Sandy achieved at these small seminars was converting seminar attendees into new clients. Possessing deep scar tissue from her past entrepre-neurial odyssey, Sandy knew she could save these women months and years of time by helping them to avoid spending too many "mistake" dollars.

The modest profits Sandy earned in her second year in this enterprise were not flashy. She was only able to pay herself about ¾ of her earnings after about 4 years into her software business. Yet she was satisfied with that since her venture was so young and she felt she was helping so many.

She counted a clientele of about 20 active clients most of the time. Some were one-off hourly consulting gigs and some had retained Sandy for the long term, paying some form of deferred fees to their mentor. Still others would retain her in cash fees for three to six months on a very part-time basis.

The mentor's true payback however was the group of

friends and contacts she was building. These were women who were longing for something more in their occupational lives and had found the spark of that with Sandy. They became extended family in a lot of cases. Sandy knew she was adding value to others, many of whom just wanted some kind of profitable side business.

One of the women in Sandy's regular Thursday golf foursome started a firm which competes with the blowhard who helped send Sandy into the mentorship business. The "self made millionaire" knows this and sends repeated cold glares toward Sandy's client from clear across the club house restaurant. He looks worried and Sandy likes it that way.

ॐ

For resources which were helpful to Sandy,
please see **www.growmedia.com**.

# 9

# Moving On Up Via Internal Reinvention

## Sales VP Bruce Becomes a Business Analyst

*Paul,*

*Here's my story of how I changed careers. If my story is of interest to you, feel free to use it. Maybe it will help someone else.*

*Best Regards,*
*Bruce P.*

Rising up to the level of Senior VP of Sales for a large office equipment company was a great ride. It was great until the day I was "encouraged" by my employer to take a buyout. My age added to my years of service exceeded the number 60 so their package would pay me $3,000 a month until my pension plan would start paying me at age 65. That was 8 years away.

This bridge compensation didn't even come close to

replacing my former comp package. But the other option was to keep working for my employer and therefore be subject to a layoff which could occur "randomly" and "without any separation package."

Talk about being a target! If I turned down the offer I may as well have painted red and white circles on my back. Needless to say I was smart enough to stick with a bird in hand rather than go for two in the bush.

Large companies these days offer separation packages to mostly please shareholders and convince them they are proactively cutting costs. But what is really behind these buyouts is their ability to get us folks to sign agreements that say we will not or cannot sue them for age discrimination!

My still profitable employer didn't care that I had raised profits in all of the regions I had worked in. I think there was also some talk about the CEO's son getting groomed for a top spot. They figured my position would get him ready for the CEO position since "Junior" had little sales background.

My attorney agreed that I had a good case, but also he helped me realize that my former employer had deeper "legal pockets" than I did. My attorney would have liked the billing time and the thrill of taking on a Fortune 1000 company, but he had my best interests at heart when he convinced me to cut and run.

At my age, the job market was brutal. I gathered many leads, networked with hundreds of friends, clients, customers, prospects, acquaintances, and I even dabbled with those social networks on the Internet. They mostly seem like a place for folks to gather who don't have anything better to do. A good resource for names and connections but they didn't help me to secure any hard job offers.

The worst economy in a generation didn't help my cause

either. Companies were cutting people and buckling down tighter than I have ever seen in my working career. I had sold around and through lots of recessions but this one was the granddaddy of them all. And it was especially hard on a fifty-something guy who was looking for work.

Finally after six months, I enlisted a career coach to help me, as I feared I was starting to look like 'damaged goods' on the street. I felt I was a well-connected guy who had strong sales skills and that I could sell myself. But so far I hadn't done so. It occurred to me I use tax professionals for my taxes and lawyers for my legal work—perhaps I should use a job coach for my occupational challenges. I wasn't desperate but I knew it was time to get some help.

We wouldn't go hungry based on my separation package, but I wanted our youngest son to be able to attend the same college the rest of the family had gone to. Financially I was stable because and my wife Leslie still had her apparently stable job.

The career coach helped me to realize that at this point in my life, I didn't really need to be "the Man" anymore. My job search had been exclusively for six-figure, sales leadership positions all over the country. I had applied for everything at the director level and VP level I could find. And this was all to no avail.

I realized how the pyramid of upper level jobs gets narrower and narrower toward the top. There is more competition for those jobs than ever due to outsourcing, a boom of Older Baby Boomers, less turnover at that level, and just plain fewer upper level jobs available—especially due to this economy. The deck seemed stacked against me.

So I began to be open to more mid-level jobs. I'd suck up my ego and get by on what those other jobs might pay. It took some time to get my head around this concept since I had been "the Man" for so many years. But with the recession as it was and my age being what it was, it started to seem that the career coach was right.

❧

A handful of employers became interested in me after I lowered my salary demands significantly. They saw a chance to land a bigger fish for a smaller fish salary. I landed a sales manager job in a non-competing industry in under four weeks. I still had to sell them on the fact that mid-range work was what I in fact wanted.

It took me a few weeks to learn the nuts and bolts of their industry which worked in the "green" space. But they too were learning as they went along since this was a new industry. The new paycheck was about half of my old one but it was nice to restart any form of compensation.

After a few months of stimulating work on that job I made another realization. I wasn't satisfied to be earning so much less than I used to, even with my bridge compensation. They had astutely asked me in the interview process why I would be satisfied to make so much less money and I had fed them some lines about "slowing down a little," and "seeking less stress." In turn they fed me lines about the "huge potential" in their business model and how "the rising tide will lift all boats."

I had kept in touch with my friends back at my former employer. The sales executives were asking me if there were any jobs at my new employer because my former employer was getting its ass handed to them by their competitors. Internet sales models were maturing and only the companies which had aggressively embraced ecommerce were surviving the recession.

Some of the Senior Level Dead Wood at my old firm had somehow survived the layoffs. Those geezers kept the company dragging well behind their industry due to their lack of innovative IT solutions. The legacy IT staff was stumped by a distributed e-commerce model simply because they only thought in terms of vertical silos. They were too isolated from both our business units and departments and our customers. The IT staff was nice enough people down in IT but their leaders had come of age in the 1970s and 1980s, and apparently it had been a decade or two since they had read an industry trade journal. Their side of the story included budgets which allowed no money for new staff or equipment.

ও

After lunch with some of my old friends to discuss my old firm's problems, I put some ideas in motion. I have been diagnosed with "idea-itis" which is a chronic case of having too many ideas to ever act on. Because of that, I made sure I put an action plan in motion.

Being in sales for so many years, I realized how customers buy based on needs, wants, ease, history, and relationships. Price is always a factor but far from the only factor. In my opinion, an effective e-commerce strategy is dependant on being customer focused. Help the buyer get what they want simply, elegantly, and cheaply, and they will beat a path to your door. Nobody in IT or the company had boiled it down that simply.

During a different lunch, this time with a couple of my C-level friends at my former employer, I got them to thinking about me. My inside knowledge plus my new "outsider" status would allow me to be the perfect outsourced solution for their ecommerce woes. I didn't posture myself as an IT person. I postured myself as a consultant who knows THEIR sales processes and dilemmas and how I could bring in a BUSINESS driven ecommerce solution to slow their declining market share. I took a day off my "day job" at the green company to spend some time with the president and one of my other friends. Due to my many years with the company, I had strong insider knowledge over other consulting companies that were also knocking on their door. My potential client learned how I could go part-time as a consultant so they could control costs and assignment length.

I got the bid because of the reputation and relationships I had in place. Since it was just me and two part-time ecommerce gurus my nephew knows, we also undercut by half any competing, multi-million dollar fees suggested by highbrow consulting firms or the brand name computer hardware or software vendors. Those guys pitched everything and the kitchen sink but we won based on trust and on my pledge to have our people MENTOR their staff rather than us bring in dozens of high paid people to do the work. I realized we'd be fighting some real legacy and political battles but the president was committed to this. His ass was on the line too!

My new green employer was thrilled I wanted to go part time with them. They were having their own cash flow issues. They were fine with me switching to only about 15 hours a week. They were even more eager to not have to pay me the small salary they were paying. They were still waiting for that tide to come in.

Somehow the departments at my client had become so segmented that they fought basic communications. But after just two weeks on the project, I encouraged the president to create mixers, buddy systems, and "Adopt a Geek" programs in order to create Forced Corporate Desegregation. We moved to quickly integrate the physical location of the IT department in and with the various business units. The moves were symbolic but critical to get everyone thinking on the same page. I felt a bit like a matchmaker after interviewing so many folks and introducing them to others who they HAD to learn to collaborate with.

Due to the movement and physical shakeups and improved communication, everyone knew the company's survival was on the line in the changing market. Gone were the days when most of the corporate office folks were ticking off their days until their fat retirement.

My nephew and his cronies soon converted to full time status under me. I didn't want to mess around with payroll so I ran their billing and paycheck through a local staffing firm for just a minor markup.

My nephew Peter was swamped with work, but as directed by me, constantly forced the work back on to the current IT staff. We had won the bid based on this model and by outsourcing as little work as possible to my team, we were building enthusiasm, productivity and morale internally. The president liked that.

He extended my contract as an independent vendor to his company. It looks like we'll be migrating and upgrading the firm's systems with and through their existing staff for several years to come. I brought in some technical trainers to help upgrade the firm's talent base. That again flagged our intent to add internal value.

I am still not half as technical as the people I work around and I never want to be. My value-add to my former employer and my present client is still from a *sales* point of view and that is why this project will succeed—it is driven by business needs. It is quite simple really...ask the *right*, strategic questions of the people on the front lines of a business, and then *listen to* and *act on* the answers.

By using my past background and industry knowledge, I was *able* to see and act on my client's internal problems. A few months apart from them helped me see things I may not have seen if I had kept my job in my silo niche there so reinventing myself really worked out.

ॐ

See the websites which helped Bruce
at www.growmedia.com.

# 10

# Go With Your Passion

## Purchasing Agent Ned Swings into a Niche

G olf is my life! Kathy and I are "empty-nest" parents and she is very busy with her work and social calendar. Therefore, golf occupies a good chunk of my life. And when my former employer laid me off nearly two Christmases ago, they implied that I spent too much time golfing. My work had saved them millions of dollars through my strategic purchasing skills, but in the end, they didn't notice or care.

Officially, I was "laid off" but it felt like a termination. They justified the layoff with the fact they were "tightening their belt," *plus* my "short hours" at the office. I do admit how I would duck out of the office around 3:30 most days but I also got in earlier than all of my peers who rarely saw that. After so many years on the job I am faster than anyone in the department. But, if the truth be told, my job at that mid-market manufacturing company was really a bore anyway.

My only severance package was two months' worth of

pay. After twelve years of work for that company! But, we can squeak by financially because both my kids opted for military duty rather than college. They can get some great tuition assistance by working for Uncle Sam and I am proud of their service. I had a good run with the US Navy just as Vietnam was wrapping up.

Despite Kathy's dream of upgrading to a nicer home like all of her friends did, I managed to talk her out of it. We don't do a whole lot of entertaining at home—most of our social activities revolve around the country club. My many years in purchasing departments helped me learn much about cash, cash flow and finance. Most of our friends have houses twice the size and up to three times the price of our little rambler, but it was sure nice to have made our last mortgage payment before I was laid off.

Kathy's income as an administrative assistant therefore covers our very basic needs so I am lucky. Most of the people laid off with me have heavy mortgages so I don't know what they are going to do. Our mid-sized North Carolina city doesn't have that many higher paying jobs. The tourism we get as a golfing destination helps the economy but it doesn't create upper-level corporate positions.

Our finances then won't allow for any travel and we had better stay healthy or else. I walk a ton on the course and my weight and cholesterol are in great shape. We were planning on moving back to Kathy's native Arizona after our retirements. We were saving up for a place in a great golf community there but with my layoff, that plan is on hold.

For awhile I worked hard to find a new job in my field. I learned that age discrimination is widespread. But, my resume showed I can save companies real money in this day and age, so I did get two interviews. Lots of time in the sun has made my face look a little older than my current fifty-eight year age. That hurt me when I interviewed for jobs and competed against younger, better-looking candidates. I know because after my interviews, the dialog with those potential employers stopped cold. I learned through my personal network how both jobs were filled with men who were in their thirties.

A bigger barrier to getting hired at my age is my senior-level wage. Due to my thirty-four years of work experience I have moved into a nice income level. But those earnings labeled me as "too expensive" I am quite sure. The job-hunting game was no fun.

⫯

One day during my job hunting efforts, I looked around my home office at my vast collection of golf-related magazines, books, toys, videos, trophies, software, and décor. Then I stared back at the computer to see some boring "me too" type of job posting which I was unlikely to get anyway. And then it hit me.

I love, know, live, and breathe golf. It is my passion and it is the growing passion of millions of people—especially people who have discretionary income and who are nearing retirement age. Right then and there I decided to earn my living with *something* related to golf.

At the time, I had no idea how I would do that but my new direction gave me a tremendous surge of enthusiasm. I stayed up almost all night researching things and writing a very informal business plan on two pads of legal paper. Based on my decades of purchasing department experience I had become an expert at acquisition. And I determined I would use that skill in the golf industry.

My new business specializes in bringing superior golf "equipment and experiences" to the upscale golfer. There are over 400 MILLION hits on Google when one searches for "golf," so sorting through all that clutter is impossible. Time-strapped, well-heeled buyers need *me* to sort through that for them.

Using my manufacturer-relations skills, I used the Internet to contact over two hundred of the best vendors of golf equipment, software, clinics, travel, workshops, memberships, and events. I offered to *contract* with them to promote their products and services to my elite clientele. My proposal to them was to simply be an independent rep that put my buyers directly in touch with the seller. That is how I would earn a commission.

Many vendors already operated using this Manufacturer's Representative model. As long as they had no exclusive territory issues, they were eager to have an informed, savvy, rep promoting them on a commission-only basis. Some of my "lines" prevented me from calling directly retailers or pro shops, yet others encouraged it. My purchasing background helped me survive this vendor maze. I am not a sales guy. I hate making any kind of sales call. But, I have elected to only represent products or services which I firmly believe in. So, I just act as the extrovert I normally am who just talks about products and services I like. There are no cold calls this way!

It took me six months to line up most of the corporate relationships and contracts with these products and services vendors. During those six months, we did dip into our Arizona house fund to pay for the legal, promotional, contractual and vendor-related travel expenses that I needed to provide for this venture. Kathy was mostly behind me on this because she saw the potential of it and was thrilled at my excitement level.

I no longer had to escape a job I hated by fleeing to the golf course. She actually sees more of me than ever and we seem to be more in love now than we have been in years. It doesn't matter where we retire now because she doesn't feel the pressing need to be near her sisters anymore. Now she has me and is no longer a golf widow. And her golf handicap is improving to the point where she is beating most of the women in her age group at the club. I'm not a bad coach!

The most enjoyable part of this venture is my ongoing "research." This includes clinics, camps, retreats, and clubs that sometime give me their new products or occasionally send me through their experiences so I know what I am representing on their behalf. What "drudgery" to put up with these lovely, elite golf experiences without having to pay a dime!

Part of my income is from being an "Elite Golf Experiences Broker." I have been invited to attend some weeklong or weekend exclusive golf experiences I would have never been able to afford in my life. Three of these golf vacation destinations have become my clients! They have me come out (most of them pay the travel costs) once a year to keep me fresh on their new offerings and features. I keep sending customers their way. A tough life!

&

My niece Anne is an information technology student who is working on her master's degree in that field. She built me a simple yet elegant web site. I can just drive my buyers to my site which then links my visitors to my clients' web sites. Amazon.com and lots of other sites have these kinds of Affiliate Programs. When my customers browse my site and click on a book or a driver or a rain suit I have recommended, they go Amazon.com or one of my other of my partners' stores. When they buy, I get a nice commission deposited directly into my account. Life is good!

Anne has talked at me for hours about how she has me "Search Engine Optimized" and I still have no idea what that means. I keep getting an occasional online payment from Google for something about "Words" or "Google Ad Words or something," but I have no idea what she's talking about. I just let her do her thing and I like how the deposits keep hitting my business checking account.

She says the architecture (I thought that was for buildings and houses) of the site is no different than other sites, but my content is what drives my high number of web site hits. She says my blog (a type of public email, I feel) is "rich in content and popular amongst industry enthusiasts in the higher net-worth demographic." Once again, I think she just means I love to chat about my favorite topic online, and that people with money to spend tend to join in.

Anne has also set me up for "Tweets" on Twitter.com. These are short little messages that come to my mobile phone if I "follow" various golf fans that are "out there." I just typed the word "golf" in their search box and I am exposed to hundreds of enthusiasts. I plan to set up Hole In One Club and a Birdie Club so people can Tweet to the world when they have a fun outcome like that. This will be like being present in the 19th Hole bar at hundreds of country clubs and golf courses all around the country. A great way to build relationships! I can "re-tweet" their good news and my community just keeps growing.

She keeps using my web site and its upgrades for college credit in her program and I hear she's getting good grades for it. She is a golfer and I pay her with the latest and greatest equipment my clients give to me for free. Don't tell her!

These Facebook.com and Myspace.com things and a few other golf-related social networking sites also seem to fuel lots of traffic to my blog I built using WordPress.com. I get to generate traffic and clicks for my clients who pay me when my surfers buy from them. I won't stare at a computer for more than three hours a day, but that time on my emails, tweets, social networks and blogs seems to drive a very steady stream of traffic to my clients.

ૐ

I visit and hang out at about two dozen courses and clubs in our golf-rich region. I start conversations with strangers easily by asking where they are from or something about where they are from or I'll inquire about that Big Bertha in their golf bag. Those conversations often lead to my handing out my card and I often learn where these 'fish" work. Then I'll hand them a bag of five nice golf tees which have my web site address only on them. I'll say something like,

> "Say, check out how the COO (a person who is from a similar kind of employer as my prospect) from XYZ Company recently enjoyed an elite golf weekend at (appropriate golf destination name here). You can read how he liked it through my blog." Ninety percent of the time people want to hear more. Everyone is out to have a good time on the golf course and they are upbeat. But I do a very "soft sell" and always am the first to end the conversation.

My personal network from the old days is very helpful too. I always kept a book filled with the thousands of manufacturing reps and salespeople who have worked with me in Purchasing Departments over the years. I was always nice to all of them and always returned their calls. Ironically, I often ended talking with those people about golf, so those relationships turned into hundreds of leads for me.

Sales reps also use golf to grease the wheels of their sales process. They were always out on the links with CEOs CFOs CIOs COOs and the like. Those reps who called on me are sort of my reps now. They always have my golf tees with them or my business cards with them to freely hand out to their connections. They do that because I give them free equipment to gain their "focus group" opinions.

My vendor clients are constantly shipping me free samples of products. And I do promote the products I believe in. But, I can't keep all that equipment so my Manufacturer's Rep Army gets those freebies! It is amazing how much good will is generated from the gift of a $400 driver.

❧

After one year of doing this, my product commissions and golf destination affiliation fees have made this venture profitable. The money is more than half what I made in my company job, but self-employment is subject to broadly inconsistent income swings. I can't recommend this type of life for anyone who needs a big, regular paycheck. But news of my success is spreading and I am getting known in this unique niche. Two product companies have contacted me regarding some form of ongoing retainer and we are discussing that. I won't get tied up in anything that feels like a job though—that would ruin all my fun. Cash flow is up and down but I predict that my second full year at this will see me net more than my old salary level. My income seems to build each month.

One interesting deal I have in the works involves a golf event for senior executives from a company that used to call on me at my former employer. Despite the tough economy, they are having a good year in their health care field. They are planning a celebration retreat for twelve of their execs as a "reward trip."

I connected this group with one of my "golf destination resort" clients and I would net thousands of dollars in commissions if that deal goes through. This business is just too much fun!

My goals are being realized because I am having fun and I have not had to dip into our nest egg except for that one time. I couldn't ask for a better way to earn a living because my work revolves around a sport I love and I get to help others build their enjoyment of the game. I wish I had been laid off sooner! I love my new vocational field, or should I say 'course' I have taken!

ॐ

To see the web sites which were helpful to
Ned, go to **www.growmedia.com**.

# 11

# Listen To Your Inner Voice

## Finance Pro Mary Goes Musical

*Paul,*

*Feel free to use my letter to Janet if you like.*

*Mary*

&bull;

Dearest Janet,

Merry Christmas to you! I hope your family is doing well. I look forward to your annual Christmas letter and I am sending mine early since so many good things have happened to me this year!

Last March, I was laid off from the job where I worked for nearly 15 years. My gas pipeline company employer reorganized and my accounting functions were shifted from our regional office down to corporate in Texas. They didn't have a position for me in Texas and they gave me a nice severance package of six months of pay due to my longevity there. But, even with a boost like that, job-hunting at age 48 is not a fun thing.

I don't think that I am eccentric but I did get some funny looks during most of my six interviews. I was never a "dress for success" type and I guess it showed. HR and the hiring managers kept looking at my appearance as if I were from Mars. I am an individual and went on these interviews dressed as my normal and unique self. I never had one negative comment about my eclectic wardrobe all the years I was with the pipeline. And furthermore, I don't believe in coloring my hair, so I guess my streaks of grey didn't meet the approval of all those dyed blonde corporate types I met.

Oh, it may have been my age or salary expectations but the bottom line is that I don't apparently fit into the new corporate America. I know because after six interviews, I had collected zero offers! That was odd since I have twenty-five years of work experience in the bookkeeping and accounting field and the firms I interviewed at all appeared to have actual open positions.

I really hated the impersonal nature of job hunting through all those Internet web sites that take up to two hours to fill out. Just let me TALK to the person who does the hiring already! I can do the darn job and I don't want to show them how well I can "fit into their work environment or culture" with some personality test.

Fortunately my severance pay allowed me to keep searching for several months. The time off work also allowed me to pursue my true passion. You have heard me tell how I was never quite good enough to make the cut as a professional symphony performer but I am still a wannabe after all these years. I love being immersed in the music scene just like when you and I were in orchestra at college!

ॐ

To fill in time while I searched for jobs, I started volunteering at the symphony offices. The deep recession was negatively affecting the symphony and they countered that with a big membership drive and promotional campaign. Their pitch was that during bad economic times people needed a higher purpose and a calming escape from the ugly realities of the stock market, foreclosures and high unemployment. There are still high net worth people around during bad times, and the arts group in our city seems to know that.

During this big drive they welcomed more volunteer hands to assist with stapling, mailing, phones, and blogging. They even had me trolling for Friends of the Symphony on FaceBook.com and LinkedIn! I got the idea about being a "professional volunteer" from Suzy at church. You met her once a couple of summers ago—she is that cello player. Anyway, hers was great advice as it got me out of the house.

The symphony office had to lay off two of its office staff during this downturn so they were always behind administratively. My volunteering expanded to twenty hours a week.

While there I noticed their main accounting software package was outdated and inefficient. I suggested a simple upgrade to the president who wanted to spend no new money. I assured him we could get it at a student rate at the local university bookstore since so many of the symphony performers were in or even teaching graduate school. The big discount moved him into the "yes" column.

My upgrade went in very smoothly since I had done this kind of thing in my sleep at the pipeline. It really helped their Accounts Payables and Accounts Receivables but even more important was the impact this project had on donations. My suggestions also included rewording of the fundraising letters (I have been a donor for years), the use of online billing statements, and the concept of "spreading out" donations via ongoing direct banking withdrawals. They implemented most of my ideas and I was a busy beaver there, volunteering up to thirty hours a week most of the time. I got so involved I forgot to keep looking for a job which actually included a salary.

Those financial controls and improvements plus the online membership social networking recruiting push (which wasn't my idea) helped membership grow by 17%! We improved fundraising to a record new level in just four months' time—even during the recession!

Because of the new levels of revenue and optimism, the board allowed the president to create a full-time, paid position for me! The pay was just over half of what I earned in my former job. And, the general office work and financial bookkeeping work is not as challenging as I was used to. But guess what? I LOVE my work and I would laugh at anyone who suggests I am moving "Down the Career Totem Pole."

I accepted the position immediately because I had felt more alive in my four-month period as a volunteer than I had in my time with my previous employer. With some significant adjustments, I have been able to get by on the salary they offered. I had already cut back on shopping, lunches out, and gift giving. I sold my nice car at a profit on EBay and now drive a paid-for bomb. Being an accountant I had always been conservative and that has really paid off for me during this switch. I don't have a huge overhead so I am now able to be part of something I love!

My work gives me contact with the symphony's board

of directors who are all high-powered businessmen and women in the community. Two of them noticed and praised my work and told me to be in touch with them at their companies when I "finish my time with the symphony."

I don't see that happening any time soon though because I love going to work each day. I am so into this job. I occasionally drag out my cello at home and play along with the recordings of the classics. I always close the window blinds though!

I look forward to your Christmas letter and the pictures of your kids. I hope you can travel home this year so I can show you around the symphony hall and my new career stop.

Peace,
Mary

ॐ

To see websites which were helpful to
Mary, see **www.growmedia.com**.

# 12

# Build on Your Marketable Skills

## Machinist Tom Retools into Consulting

The family's small, Midwestern hog farm didn't generate enough income for any extras. Tom's mother's job
in town helped hold things together for them but provided
no luxuries. As a result of growing up in that situation,
Tom and his brother learned how to fix everything that
broke. Their farm equipment was less than modern and
the boys and their dad became the best repair guys around
by necessity. Sometimes their repairs actually consisted
of using just duct tape and bailing wire!

After high school, Tom joined the military to get away. In
the Marines, he tested out highly in mechanical aptitudes.
He was assigned to several mechanic and equipment shops
during his time in the service. He flourished, but returned
to his Midwestern roots after a very positive four-year stint.
His pickup was laden with "Semper Fi," "US Marines," and
USA flag stickers.

He returned to his hometown but not the farm. My

grandfather was happy to hire Tom to work in his one-person machine shop. Grandpa's 62 years made it harder and harder for him to do the heavy physical work required. They repaired farm equipment and created custom tools for a few small plants around the area. Tom worked with Grandpa by day and took night courses over at the technical community college.

Tom was smart as a whip and incredibly innovative with his head and hands. He had seen a lot in his tour of duty and combined that with his high intellect and now the academic training. Grandpa said Tom did the work of two men. Grandpa's customers all heard about Tom's high capability. Even though I was just 8 years old at the time, I remember Grandpa bragging about Tom to the guys at the coffee shop. I wanted to be just like Tom when I grew up!

The shop's reputation and business grew so Grandpa hired a couple of part-time, after-school teenagers to help Tom out. Those extra hands were needed because at the time crop prices were forcing farmers to hang on to their equipment longer. And some regional businesses were using Grandpa's shop for more and more work. The coffee shop men teased Grandpa when he announced that he was buying fancier tools and expanding the size of the shop. Tom became a 30% owner after his first year.

Tom graduated from the community college's tool-and-die program and convinced Grandpa to grow more. They added onto the west side of the shop and Tom was the General Contractor. His relatives helped out with the construction which was the biggest building project our small town had seen in quite awhile.

Tom visited area manufacturing plants, studied their needs and usually came up with a low-cost, homegrown solution that enhanced their production. Tom impressed more than one "educated" engineer.

After two more years, over two-thirds of the business came from the tool making and custom equipment building side of the business. Tom's clients often sought his advice when they were doing some of their typical retooling. Since their production needs and product lines kept changing, they often had to retool themselves relatively often.

After four years Tom was a 50/50 partner with Grandpa who wanted to quit and sell the whole business to Tom. Grandpa had really only been working in a part-time, public relations role but Tom insisted that the Founder's role was valuable for getting new business.

Tom's problem was that he had no lump sum or decent credit to buy out Grandpa's share. So, they worked out a deal where Tom would pay Grandpa over a ten year period. Grandpa insisted Tom was the reason for the shop's success so accepted only a *modest* settlement for his half. Everyone was happy.

છ

Tom had gotten married to Brenda, his high school sweetheart. They started a family immediately. He grew the shop over the years into a full-blown, tool and die shop with specialized clients all over the region.

I went on to become an aircraft mechanic for a major corporation in Memphis and worked there for 15 years. Eventually I got laid off in a major cost cutting spree which hit when jet fuel prices reached record highs. That recession had caused a major slowdown in the shipping industry.

છ

Many years passed and Tom and Brenda's boys were in the military and college. Tom wanted to sell out, retire, and see the "world" with his bride via an RV. I bought the shop which now had eight, highly-skilled employees. History repeated itself as Tom sold me the shop and agreed to owner-financing. He remembered me being the kid who hung around his grandpa's shop, so he cut me a good price.

Tom and Brenda traveled for most of a year. His emails from the road told me how he visited not only the Grand Canyon and the Everglades, but many small manufacturing plants and tool and die shops all over the country. It is a good thing Brenda likes to read!

After his travels were complete, Tom was itching to get busy again. I invited him to attend a specialty trade conference with me in Kansas City. That really got his juices flowing and he was like a kid in a candy shop.

At the conference I introduced him to people who used to sell equipment, tools, and services to me and my team at the big shop in Memphis. These were real machine guys and they hit it off with Tom over beers. Based on my introductions, Tom's reputation, likeability and smarts, those friends also introduced him to other key players in the industry.

Tom gathered up many business cards, brochures and booklets about new technology and design and equipment issues in the sector. He even snuck into a couple of seminars which were aimed at engineers.

After the trade conference, I knew Tom would never last as an early retiree. He chatted regularly with his new contacts. Being a quick study, he determined, in just a few months, new ways to serve that tool industry niche. His innovative mind and big-picture vision helped him decide to become a *consultant* to the tool industry. He thought that sounded too lofty a title to put on his new business card. He just said that he "specializes in talking to people about their production, repair and design problems." Then he comes up with solutions. He offered his ideas to them on a contingency basis—the client would pay Tom for his ideas *if in fact they chose to implement them.*

This pricing structure got him in the door many times as with potential clients. Most of the time, he expended a fair amount of work and got no paycheck for the ideas he put forward. On a few other occasions he was actually paid a very nice fee for the cost-effective solutions he offered on a contingency basis. His market niche was small-town manufacturers or mid-sized firms in the region. Income wasn't important to him at that point in his life, as he just wanted to stay busy and use his creative mind. As long as he still had time for hunting and fishing.

Of course Tom has his own workstation area in my shop. He often drops by for some hands-on tinkering to test an idea, or when he just gets tired of staring at his computer at his home office. The shop guys like it when he shows up because it adds a creative energy to the place.

For me, things feel like they have come full circle because my 10-year old son hangs out at the shop a lot. Whenever Tom shows up, my son wants to know so he can hang out and watch. He sits on the same metal bench my Grandpa made for me!

❧

To see Internet resources helpful to Tom, go to
www.growmedia.com.

# 13

# Listen for Hidden Opportunities

## Fast-Track Sales VP Goes Financial

When I started work at the IT consulting company in the early 1990s, we were just a handful of sharp people with good ideas, vision, and great timing. In just seven years, Mike's company bootstrapped its way to a company with branch offices in eight Southeastern cities. Our company's revenues approached $25 Million. Life was very hectic but fun and profitable.

As employee number five with the company, I prospered. I was named National Sales manger and all client relationships ultimately reported up to me. I was *the* top rainmaker and earned over $275,000 in compensation during my best years with the firm.

Then we hit some obstacles. The demand for IT consulting services was slowing, project work replaced some IT contractors, national players had noticed our success and had moved into our markets, the first wave of "e-business" had come and gone, and clients were sending more and more work offshore. Plus, the talent shortages which we had cashed in on were shrinking. It was a supply and demand business and the colleges had turned out more, lesser expensive supply of talent.

Our attempts to reinvent ourselves didn't work well. We tried to go with the times and become an "ecommerce" consultancy, but revenues slipped and Mike grew restless. Over the years, I had always been focused on negotiating better annual compensation and bonuses for myself. I had always achieved good income growth so I had neglected to focus on stock or stock options with Mike's firm. I had assumed the gravy train was going to keep going and had been too naïve to ask for a chance to get or buy some ownership.

Also, I thought Mike would own the firm forever and pay me well since I was his key guy. But, I was dead wrong. One day, he announced that he had signed a letter of intent to sell the company. I couldn't breathe! My personal overhead was high so I was in a risky situation. My wife and I liked nice things and had enjoyed some Irrational Exuberance during the Red Hot 90's.

The buyer of Mike's company was a bigger player in the industry and they had their own national sales manager. After just two months, they let me go with a severance package of six months of my base income. We could and did stretch that to a year's worth of safety net by immediately cutting back on everything and liquidating some investments, fortunately before the crash of '01. We kept asking ourselves how we had gotten so stupid about spending.

ॐ

So, it was off to the job market I went. I interviewed with several companies that discussed offering me less responsibility and less money. Mike was fat and happy but I couldn't find a job that paid half of my former peak earnings. I was concerned about keeping at least some of *my creditors* "in the lifestyle to which they had become accustomed." I had nearly one thousand personal business contacts in southern California but not one of them converted into a realistic job offer! The IT consulting market was changing and leaving me behind.

I met with my financial services representative regarding 401K issues. I needed to roll it over now that I was a former employee, and I was considering taking some of that money to keep things floating on the home front. Steve showed me the stupidity of *that*. He seemed so calm and collected even though many of his customers were suffering in the recession. I asked him how he kept his head about him in crisis and he said just one word: "Planning."

His demeanor stuck with me long after our meeting. I called him up for lunch in order to chat with him about his work. Steve heard how my job search was going poorly and he was sympathetic. Then he surprised me by asking me to consider joining his company.

I had always viewed myself as a business-to-business sales person. I didn't know much about doing business-to-consumer sales and didn't think I would like it. I'm best at big time RFPs and board room PowerPoint presentations and all that. But, when you have no job, you listen to all leads.

Steve's firm actually had 2 representatives who actually made more than I did at my peak earnings at Mike's firm. Those two guys had each been in the industry for about twenty years so I was told to be realistic *if* I decided to pursue this. When meeting them I realized Steve's guys were sharp like me. I immediately felt I could do that job and started visualizing myself doing so.

After thinking about things for a long time and doing some extensive research, I felt I had found a "brand-name," national scope company that was interested in me and interested in having me earn a large, no-limits income in a territory which I would create and control. I hadn't found that any other employer who had those attributes. So I bit.

I passed their interviews, whizzed through their structured training programs, and weeks later, aced the Series 7 and similar tests required to sell investments and insurance. Selling insurance products and financial services, offering fee-based planning, and brokering securities is an exciting idea for me. This is because my former sales world was comprised typically of corporations which had some size to them, say 100+ employees on the very low end. Many cities had only 50 or 60 companies in their whole metro which could be potential clients of our services. Now, my range of service allowed me to have *everyone* as a potential client of mine. New graduates from college as well as high-net worth technology millionaires, and everyone in between were all prospects for me.

Another feature I view as a plus in the financial services sector are the renewals that contribute to a representative's income. In IT contracting, we had ongoing revenue (and commissions) for the life of the clients' projects only. In the financial services business, I will get renewal commissions for many years if I apply my customer service skills and keep my clients happy. This supplemental source of ongoing income is very attractive. On the securities side, I choose to provide services on managed-fee basis. This allows me to focus on my clients' big-picture needs.

My one thousand-plus contacts were critical to my fairly

quick start in this business. My ramp-up *did* take nearly a year despite those connections and my talent. But I have learned a ton and I really believe I can help anyone. That passion drives my success and I have been recognized by our company and a "Fast Starter to Watch." I am in the top ten percent of producers nationally for people at my tenure in the business.

My background in technology services has helped my success. I use several social networks, especially **www.linkedin.com**, plus email alerts, RSS feeds, blogs, Podcasts, and webinars (both to teach and to learn). I am now tied to technology more than I ever was while I was in the technology business!

I carry the latest Bluetooth Blackberry device everywhere. I get Tweets (messages no longer than 140 characters) via Twitter at least 25 times a day. On Twitter I follow and am followed by about 100 people who want to hear strategic, up-to-the-minute financial advice. It is a great credibility and client builder for me.

So, I am in individualized contact with *at le*ast two dozen current and potential clients *every day*. Other reps in our office just sit and shake their heads at the volume of connections and messages. They call me *The Networking Cyborg*. Steve has already given me a full-time office assistant.

My success in this industry is *not* because I know a few technology millionaires. I only have one of them for a client. Instead of millionaires, I have dozens of Starbucks Baristas as clients, for example. I work every person I can work and those Starbucks clerks got started with me because I started relating to them via Twitter. Even though they don't make too much money, many of them are now in their early twenties and have financial planning needs.

I keep fueled via a gallon of coffee and/or Diet Coke a day. The local Starbucks drive-through has my photo on their Hall of Fame wall. The other day I actually went inside that store. There I ran into a former co-worker who was a peer of mine at Mike's firm.

When he heard I was a financial services rep, he groaned and said he was glad he hadn't had to stoop to *that* level yet. He was currently between jobs since his first stop in commercial real estate hadn't worked out.

I kept my cool and calmly told him approximately how much income I was on track for that year. Then I named a couple of big shots he knew who "were typical" of my clientele. While he stood there with his mouth hanging open I bought him the most expensive Starbucks drink I could find on the menu. When I left he was still speechless.

I am glad I discovered this hidden opportunity which was under my nose the whole time!

ॐ

To see web resources which were helpful to Frank, go to **www.growmedia.com**.

# 14

# Helping Other Helps You

## Bored Executive Bob Joins Boards

*Paul,*
   *As per your request about my "successful semi-retirement timeline," see below.*

*Regards,*
*Bob*

**July:**
   After all those years with the firm, I wanted to slow down. I've reached the level of Assistant VP of Finance at our Fortune 1000 conglomerate. I couldn't believe it was thirty-five years ago I started as a Staff Accountant Trainee. Over three decades later my boss and friend the CFO encouraged me to take the nice separation package that was being offered. He and I had worked together for many years and he suggested that I work too hard. He plans to be leaving in the next two years himself so he thought now was a good time for me, early pension and all, to "make a break for it."

I'm easily eligible for the early pension under the terms of the proposal. That plan will more than cover our living expenses since we are senior empty nesters. There isn't much mystery left in my job, I didn't want to try move up anymore—they have younger guys for that kind of chase. Plus, the economy is hitting our construction industry already. It was time to get out while the "getting was good."

However, I'm not opposed to continuing to earn a good income. I am used to that and the more I make, the more we can help the kids. Plus there are a couple of really expensive trips Beth wants to take, and we aren't willing to touch our nest egg for those costs.

Also, I'm not yet 60 so I want to stay active and keep the gray-matter functioning.

Starting or buying a business isn't interesting to me. I have always worked for big companies and I don't want to play around with a little one. I am a specialist and am not really interested in doing all parts of a small enterprise. And I don't like the idea of having to be a Willie Loman and sell my services. Nor do I want to be an absentee owner of some business which might go bust and harm our long term investments. Although I have heard that a laundromat owner can really clean up!

**October:**

Our trips to Rio and Greece were fantastic. The tour companies spoiled us rotten and I loved reconnecting with my bride of 36 years.

As great as the trips were, you still have to come home. After hanging out for a few months it just seems to get quieter and quieter around the house. Beth had a full social calendar so it is just the dog and I hanging around. I do the treadmill and the business news in the morning, wonder what I'm going to have for lunch, and then end up taking an hour nap or so in the afternoon while waiting for Beth to wrap up her social and charitable events of the day. Then we grill out or go out and wind down. We have some church and social activities in the evening a couple of times a week, but this seems too much like *full* retirement! And I didn't like it.

I was asked by a friend at church to serve as board member for a prominent non-profit organization. Joel knew I was a bit bored and the timing was perfect. It is an honor to be asked to join this group. Executives in town typically seek out this type of appointment due to its high visibility. They like to build their community service resumes that way. I'm joining for none of those reasons. I believe in this cause *and* I'm just glad to get out of the house.

The board meets once a month but I serve on the finance committee which meets a time or two each month outside of the main board meeting. The meetings remind me of some of the snoozers I sat through at the office for all those years, but it is nice to meet new people and help out this worthy cause.

**November:**

This charity does a great job serving its clientele, but they sure need some better financial controls. Other folks on the board know help is needed but didn't have time to spend overhauling the financial processes of the group. And it really isn't their *job* to do that. There is a full-time, paid finance department in place. Since I have the time and the ability to help, I offered my services.

There was some turf war resistance to my suggested changes, but, the recommendations were approved at the committee level and I was set up to work with and through the paid staff for about a month, part-time. This will get things onto a more modern track.

It would have cost the charity $250 an hour to bring in the level of talent that I bring for free. The Executive Director knew that so he forced this through his staff with a velvet hammer. It was nice to be needed.

**January:**

While serving on this board I met a man named Rafael. He is the CEO of a privately-held, 1,500-employee company based here in New York State. He was impressed by my direction of the charity's finance project and asked me to serve on his company's corporate Board of Directors.

I agreed to join him and was especially happy to later learn this assignment pays an annual stipend of $12,000. *And*, this board holds one of their meetings at an exotic Caribbean resort! Beth and I and the other board members and their guests all attend at the expense of the company! Rafael's business is doing well and he takes care of his leadership.

**March:**

After Raphael's board meeting in St. Thomas, I realized my skills might be a foot in the door to other profitable, non-traditional "jobs." After getting to know some of the other board members and at their encouragement, I considered the idea of making a second career of being a professional board member. The work was casual, occasional, had flexible accountability, no managerial stress, it utilized my expertise, and it even paid well in most cases. What's not to love?

I am researching for more opportunities to serve on the

boards of for-profit, usually mid-sized or smaller privately held firms. There were several Internet tools like Hoovers, LinkedIn.com, and Jigsaw which are my favorites. From these I can learn a ton about companies out there at no or little cost. I dig in and try to find companies which I am guessing need financial help and would therefore be interested in my background. The recession is hurting a number of industries right now but I target the ones which I am guessing are bleeding the worst. Those folks who are hurting need immediate assistance.

I don't approach them as a consultant because like I said before I don't want to become a small business man. When I find a local or regional company which fits my template, I use all my internet tools to locate someone I know who has knowledge of that firm. Then I approach my contact to see if he or she feels that company might need any new board of advisor type of talent. This is slow but the nice thing is I don't have any urgent demands. It is not like I am looking for a job and the mortgage depends on this.

Of course I always dial down toward companies where their advisors are reimbursed. But, if a firm (or a charity) is interesting to me, I'm considering being recruited for a "pro-bono" assignment.

**November:**

My "portfolio" of board of director seats has grown to 6, including 2 non-profit boards. I have not created any kind of profile on these social networking tools, but my name is listed, I suspect, on some of these Internet sites or lists that profile companies and their boards of advisors. I am listed somewhere I know because I now average an invitation every month to join someone else's board.

The rich content on the internet is amazing and word of my involvement on these boards just breeds more attention. I pop up on a lot of searches because of my former high-level position with my old brand-name employer. But this attention all surprises me a bit because the boards I sit on are all private companies. The internet has really made everything transparent—especially these social media tools.

Obviously I turn down the frequent requests to serve on boards. I need to stick with my present companies to do any good. I don't want to get too watered down or spread too thin or work too hard! And I always avoid even the perception of any potential conflict of interest regarding my board assignments.

ఎ

One thing is for sure. When you get yourself out there in a network of people and keep priming the pump with appropriate contacts, good things can happen. We didn't need the money but now my several board assignments pay more annual income than some people earn in a year. And, I can avoid working for several days in a row if I choose to!

Beth looks forward to seeing her friends again at Rafael's next warm-and toasty board event. I hear we are going to the Caymans in March!

So I keep just as busy as I want. I use my strategic financial skills to help my clients, if you want to call them that. I meet and work with interesting people, I help companies grow, and keep my mind active. It is a real win-win for all of us involved. But, my favorite board activity so far was my first seat on that non-profit. There I made a big impact on their operations and that allowed them to serve more and more people in their charity. That makes me feel good.

જી

For Internet resources that helped Bob, go to **www.growmedia.com**.

# 15

# Rearrange Your Thinking

## Sales VP Rick Heads up the River

**My career transition diary:**

**September 11**

I can't retire—I'm only 41 years old! *Someone* out there needs a seasoned, Vice President of Sales and Marketing! But, I think that I am getting automatically rejected when I complete online job applications. They ask about the salary required or expected and most of those boxes or fields on those online applications won't let you put "open" or "negotiable." They demand a number. So, I *give* them one.

I am worth a high dollar figure because I grew top-line revenues by 26% for the major two lines of our sports equipment division that I headed up. Nobody knows distribution, manufacturing, and marketing to retail better than me! That is *worth* a high salary, isn't it? Am I really too expensive?

With Jan and John in private school, and their mom working just part time, we *need* a high income. Throw in our "McMansion" and our boat and we'll be in trouble quick-like without my former income.

**November 16**

My interviews in and outside of the sporting goods industry have produced no hits. I have talked to everyone I know inside the industry and done all the social networking and blogging and all that stuff the coaches say to do. I got a couple of meaningful discussions but the industry is slow right now. Everyone is holding all their cards to their chest due to this damn recession. All the players in the field are acting like no customer anywhere is ever going to want to buy a discretionary item ever again! It is frustrating. I recommend using this slow time to get strategic and get ready for the new wave of good times!

One prospect I have is an emerging technology firm owned by a guy at the country club. Everything was cool regarding this sales job where I would get to learn a new industry. Everything was cool, that is, until they came in with an offer well under $100K. I made that 6 years ago and had to tell him I was holding out for more. I'm not sure how long I can hold out though. Everyday that goes by without a job makes me think I should call that tech company and ask if the job is still open. I don't think it is...

**December 20**

Looking back, I think I should have definitely accepted that tech firm's job offer. I was full of myself back then but things have really been slow, even during my industry's busy season.

I need to land something soon because we are dipping way too deep into our savings to get by. We have made some big cuts in our life and I got lucky by selling the boat. Even though we took a loss on it, I won't have the payments, maintenance, and slips fees anymore. We only got out on it about four or five times a year anyway! Ginger is back to work full-time and she hates it. The kids are back in public school again and seem to be coping. They both have our neighbors as schoolmates so their transitions have been pretty painless. I don't miss the tuition payments and their mother and I can fill in the religious content they are not getting at public school. When times get better they may get to go back to the private school.

Perhaps I'll be able to sort things out over our annual road trip home for the holidays. Ginger loves the small town charm back home. I love it too—it was a great place to grow up. As kids, we loved our water sports and hunting and fishing activities. Those experiences most likely birthed the passion I have for my twenty-year work history in the sporting goods industry.

On our road trip we were about an hour from our hometown when I had to pull off and scrape some ice buildup off the windshield. The window had gotten coated when we had stopped for lunch and the wipers weren't clearing it off. I pulled off in the driveway of a canoe rental/outfitter company. An older guy was digging around under the hood of an old van. I asked him if he needed a ride anywhere to which he replied,

"No, I live here," as he pointed toward the business's building which had a "For Sale by Owner" sign on the door. He told me he just had to jimmy the battery cables and he'd be fine. After reading his makeshift sign once more I blurted out,

"You selling the place then?"

"Yeah. You want to buy it?"

I was shocked by his candor and muttered something about needing to get back on the road. I started walking away but the colorful man kept me engaged in conversation for another few minutes.

Lyle and his wife Ellen were selling the river excursion/ canoe outfitter business after twenty-one years. They could no longer handle the physical demands of the enterprise and business had been slow last summer due to the economy. He told me he was asking $250,000 for everything "lock, stock, and barrel." Lyle seemed nice enough, but he came off as desperate.

His question about buying his business stuck in my brain for the final leg of our trip. There is no way I could picture my suburban family up here in the cold weather zone surrounded by nothing but pine trees and an occasional Holstein cow.

We had a great holiday with the relatives.

**January 3**

I returned home from up north to find a dozen reject emails regarding job applications I'd sent out before our trip. I purposely avoided checking emails or texts while we were home for the holidays. It was peaceful but yet it was an avoidance technique. The stress of *not* looking for work that week *bypassed* the stress of *unsuccessfully* looking for work for that period of time. .

I sent out a total of twenty-seven resumes or online job applications in November and December. About half of those HR departments were kind enough to actually let me know via email that they rejected me. Is that called a personal or an impersonal rejection?

When their ads say, "Only the most qualified will receive a response," I want to reach through the damn laptop and strangle someone. Doesn't anyone care that I *dominated* my district in 1998, 1999, and 2005? Doesn't *anyone* need a proven expert who can move a massive amount of goods? I know we are in a recession but wouldn't someone who can *sell* a company's products be needed? My attitude is slipping...

Attempts by me to work with and through CEOs, COOs, and VPs of big and medium companies have not worked. Everyone keeps saying how nobody is hiring during this recession. Ginger is concerned. *I* am concerned. We are looking into tapping our 401K for cash to be able to keep this oversized house.

After some fruitless Internet job surfing one day, I just picked up the phone and called Lyle at the canoe rental business. He remembered me from our brief meeting and we chatted for over an hour. He emailed me crude spreadsheets of his business financials for past few years.

His price for the operation includes the company's vans, trailers, canoes, canoe equipment plus the old home and storage building on almost 7 acres of wooded land. He and most rural Wisconsinites are consistently genuine.

I played with the numbers all night. Using our 401Ks, home equity, and credit-worthiness, this might be a deal which would work! Lyle and Ellen owned everything out-right, and offered to do owner financing. In his best year, Lyle's business netted less than half of my former income. But his whole operation was valued at way less than the price of our house! And we really have pretty good equity in our overpriced digs here. I didn't tell Ginger about my number crunching sessions.

**February 11**

Ginger is getting counseling about my unemployment. That makes *me* crazy because I am the one who needs help! Her folks lent us some money while I keep looking for work. Neither of us wanted us to tap into our retirement funds but our other savings are now gone. Who are those guys who get severance packages when they leave their long term employer? I got the vacation which was due to me plus just one month of pay. A raw deal...

I have one job offer that is coming soon. It will pay about 80% of my former income but we'd need to relocate from suburban Kansas City to the Dallas area. Houses there that are anywhere close to what we have here would cost 40% to 50%. A person can get into our home's payment range by commuting for an hour but that isn't the life I want to lead. Accepting this job just doesn't seem to make sense and Ginger seems to agree.

I can't get Lyle's business out of my head. But how could I convince my family to be interested?

**March 2**

Tonight I made the sales pitch to my family to buy the canoe rental business and move 'up north.' I used my best corporate presentation skills. I included benefits, risk factors, cash flow diagrams, and more. This PowerPoint presentation far exceeded my best-ever corporate dog-and-pony show.

The kids wouldn't even consider leaving their friends and their activities. I anticipated this objection and offered that we might be able to hire their pals for summer help. I also pointed out that they would meet many other kids their age in this tourist hotspot.

My son John missed the cut at his school's "semi-pro"

football team last year. I told him he might be the starting quarterback at a smaller school. Besides, he loves the Green Bay Packers.

And Jan seems to be stuck on the wrong path with her friends right now. Her peer group in public school has too many piercings, wild hair looks, and revealing clothing styles in my opinion. She doesn't seem like she's over the edge with all this yet, but it is only a matter of time for her to try to keep up with her wilder friends at the huge public school.

Ginger was very quiet. This business would mean living in a small, old house, working a million hours a week all summer, and leaving her clubs, friends, and church. She always knew her future might still require a corporate move, but this was far from corporate! The whole town where the canoe business was based has a smaller population than our subdivision!

Her grandfather died last summer so that did make her rethink her values and what was important to her for the second half of her life. Being a "corporate wife" for life was not her life's mission and she does love it back home.

I let things simmer in everyone's head for several days. I strategically kept a potential Dallas move into the conversation to keep some contrasts alive. By the end of the week, everyone was coming up with a new idea about how we could improve the canoe excursion business!

Jan thought she could meet some "cute guys" who would be customers of river excursions. John saw himself as the starting quarterback of a football team at a school where there were only 500 students in the whole place. Ginger was coming along with the concept as long as she could move our present house to the river! They were coming around! Unbelievable!

**March 18**

Lyle got my offer today via email. It is contingent upon selling our house, which has appreciated very nicely over our nine years here. We have gotten lots of interest in it even though there are several like it for sale in the neighborhood. Since we bought it right so long ago, we have solid equity and are offering a lower sale price. The strategy is working!

The home equity will make the whole canoe business deal possible combined with Lyle's generous owner-financing!

Lyle had one other suitor who is a "big city guy from Minneapolis" according to him. In Lyle's mind, this other potential buyer has no ties to Lyle's area and he'd rather deal with a "native" like me. He didn't say that but I still speak the language from up that way, *don't ya know*.

**April 25**

*The deal is done!* I feel alive! I may become a *starving* boss, but I am my *own* boss! This is empowering. Our house closes in two weeks so all the paperwork will then be complete. I am headed up to learn everything from Lyle and Ellen and get some stuff I'll need to create a web site for the business. Lyle never had one.

I can already think of fifty ways to improve this new venture. I *am* a top marketing executive, you know! Right now is prime booking season, so I am really focused on online marketing. I am going to use ecommerce to make this business the foremost outdoor excursion destination in its region!

My knowledge of equipment, marketing, the geographic area, sporting goods trends from a macro perspective, corporate groups which need team building etc. etc. etc. will blow this baby wide open—recession or no recession!

For two weeks I have gotten about 5 hours of sleep

because of my work on creating a huge virtual footprint for the business. Lyle's sleeper company was driven by word of mouth and little Yellow Page ad. I'm using hundreds of his old photographs to create a web site which has a retro feeling of "simpler times" and "family times."

The site is nothing fancy—I just bought the website templates from the registration company and plug my content into that. Anyone who can do word processing can do this—they have plug-and-play tools for non-techies like me.

Also, I am already getting attention and interest in bookings due to the business's imprint on social networking/social media sites. My angle is to create and infiltrate dozens of online special interest groups and eventually encourage the members therein to gather *in person* for one of our excursions. They use my easy online registration form and my outsourced payment/deposit system. And cash is already headed our way!

My marketing also appeals to families and family reunion groups to meet at our river instead of expensive Disneyland or cruise type of vacations. "Get back to the basics" appeals to lots of people in this economy.

It seems to be working. Lyle said he has never seen bookings this high this early. He tells me he charged me way too little for his business, now that he sees what the company is worth. I told him I will make it up to him by letting him stop by anytime to eat all the free Slim Jims he wants. Ginger says he reminds her of her dad and she has a quiet glow about all this crazy transition we are in. Her counseling sessions have stopped.

## August 11

We have never worked so hard! Everyone in the family is too busy to worry about adjusting to this new life. Due to the small house and teamwork nature of this venture, I am closer to my kids than I have been in years.

Ginger and I are also feeling closer since now my only corporate travel is to haul canoes one way or the other along the river. We rediscovered what we liked about each other way back when. You can forget those things when you do as much business travel as I used to do.

Her outlook on life seems much better and I think that is due to her feeling like she is important again. Since I used to travel so much and the kids hung with their friends she used to feel ignored. Now, we are all in this together and all we have time to feel is busy and tired. Ginger and I have both lost weight, are tanner, and stronger than ever. This has really improved our romance factor!

Lyle never told me how much work this business is. If I was paid hourly I'd be a millionaire. But he tells me I'll be stir-crazy in the quiet of January. However, I think we'll host cross country ski outings over at the state park then. Lyle just rolled his eyes when I told him that.

Jan is our webmaster because she loves that computer. She has created 1,000 or so friends of the business on Facebook. Her networking there is certain to bring back repeat customers next year—they all want to come back to see her. At least the teenaged boys do.

On weekends John plans to host a few off road bicycle tours on the public land nearby. We'll rent out our bikes and transport folks for day trips. We now offer tent camping on our own land.

Lyle and Ellen bought a little house in town and they visit us often. He is amazed at our "marketing machine" and still complains with a smile how I hoodwinked him on price. I tell him to just keep chewing his Slim Jims.

Business is steady and I have really bumped up the retail component of this place. People tend to spend money when they are in vacation mode if you make it easy and fun for them to do. And I know a lot about merchandising.

### September 7

As we wind down our first season, we should finish with net profit nowhere close to our former household income. Or you could say it is *way above* our former household income since I was earning nothing after getting laid off.

We've never worked this hard or spent this much time together. And we wouldn't trade it for the world. You get to meet some great people in this business. They are out having fun so our customers are much more fun to be around than my former corporate customers.

It seems we have more discretionary income because our costs are so low and our work is mostly fun. We don't have time or energy to go looking for entertainment. I used to drop $100 bucks at a happy hour with the guys but I haven't been to a bar in months. The kids used to blow through $200 bucks at the mall in a weekend but they don't even know what movies are out right now. We have one old paid-for minivan as the family car unless you want to count our three rickety 15-passenger vans.

Two years ago I would have called you nuts if you told me our family would love working their fingers to the bone in an old little house in the north woods. But look at us now—we love it!

℘

To learn about Internet resources which were helpful to Rick, please go to www.growmedia.com.

# 16

# Do What You Do Best

## Radio Ronnie—The Show Must Go On!

It has been a fun career. In the early 1970s I chose to study broadcasting at an area college which had a good program. After that I was in the right place at the right time and launched a career in radio.

I love radio—the talk, the music, the format strategies, the on-site promotions, etc. I loved being a "regional talent" for my music/call-in show. I got better and better at the job and after about 3 years of it I was "Red Hot Ronnie." We had the best ratings of any radio program among the most attractive demographical audience for our advertisers. At my peak, we were even getting considered for national radio syndication of my show. Our station owner had three AM stations in southern Ohio and my show was carried on all three at the same time. We dominated our time slot across ten or so counties. I earned the station lots of money because selling ads during my program was easy-cheesy.

Just as those syndication talks were getting started, they

stopped abruptly. My type of program format was dropping dead on the coasts and the national players didn't think my program's template would last more than six more months. With music moving toward the FM band and talk radio's slow emergence on AM, I was told I would soon be a relic. There I was, under thirty years old and I was about to be a "has-been!"

My boss offered me the program manager position as long as I sold airtime advertising on a "part-time" basis. At first, I was appalled to be asked to sell ads. After all, I was "Talent." But I had no other job or no other skills, so I gave it a whack. I had to have a job!

My name recognition in the region helped me get a foot in the doors at many potential advertising clients. People took my appointments or phone calls because they had heard my name before. But, I stunk as a salesman. Without any other job prospects though, I decided I had to improve at selling. I read lots of books and materials by Zig Ziglar and nearly memorized his sales training cassette tapes while driving from client to client. Over the period of three years I got pretty good at sales and actually started making my boss some money again.

I long-ago dumped the Program Manager role and earned the title of Sales Manager over all three of his stations. One day though the boss announced he had sold all three of his stations to a radio holding company and he planned to retire to Arkansas. I was worried.

The new company let me keep selling but without the Sales Manager title or responsibility. For two more years I continued to leverage all of my relationships in the area and proved to be one of the leading sales reps for the holding company. The corporate office eventually made me the Sales Manager over a dozen stations in a two state area. The money was very good and the responsibility felt right. I appreciated the steady job because I had gotten married to Marie and we had two young children fairly quickly. Life moved along like that for many years. But then 'industry consolidation' again raised its ugly head.

Our radio station holding company merged with another similar company. There was not room for my regional sales level position so I was cut. Nothing surprised me anymore. Soon to be jobless and all I knew was radio. Fortunately our debt load was low and we had saved a few months' worth of income. They laughed at me when I asked them if there was any severance package.

My on-air success had been a stroke of luck based on the times and couldn't be duplicated. I checked out real estate, insurance, executive recruiting, manufacturer's rep sales, retail management, and a couple of corporate sales manager jobs. None of those fields particularly grabbed me. I did land three interviews in those industries but must have come off as bored because none of them called me back.

While driving home from one of those interviews, I noticed a small sign on an office building. It was for a tiny Wedding DJ service. I'd never really noticed that business before and had paid little attention to them since I was a "big name" and all. The trend in wedding receptions was to have a disc jockey playing top hits on his portable equipment. It was cheaper and more controllable than having a live band at receptions. I learned more about that little DJ service over the next few days.

I turned down a new offer for an assistant manager in an office supply store. I knew I didn't want to spend my occupational life figuring out profit margins on photocopy machines and desk chairs. Marie was very supportive, and we studied the mobile entertainment industry even more. After a few weeks of intense research and planning, we decided to take the leap of faith. We planned to try our hand at using my former "celebrity" to become a *Mobile Entertainment Vendor*. We borrowed a few thousand dollars from Marie's cool dad. He always liked my show in the old days and was very supportive of the idea.

ح

We didn't know half of what we needed to know to actually succeed in this venture, but our heart was in it. We began acquiring and building used equipment, music, sales leads and "bruises."

There were many pitfalls along the way: Bad bookings, tight cash flow, travel and set-up difficulties, constant night work, music inventory issues, and rotten and even drunken crowds. Despite those difficulties, I loved what I was doing because I was entertaining people again.

The parents of some of the bridal couples remembered my show from years back and were happy to book me. I played hits right out of their coming-of-age, more carefree time and those well-established parents always tipped me lavishly.

Money was never flush until I learned how to book some daytime events. I finally figured out to call on my former corporate customer base by serving the "corporate entertainment market." On a daily basis, companies have sales, product, training, and every other kind of meetings. Most hotels in our area hosted some company or association meeting nearly every day except Sunday. These events often could benefit from a gifted Master of Ceremonies and sometimes musical support.

The city's Visitor and Convention Bureau had booking information that listed the various association meetings that were coming to town in the future. From that data, I used my outgoing personality to approach the contact people in charge of those meetings. This took some investigative work, but it has proved to be a very worthwhile source of gigs for us.

I convinced several event planners that my strategically placed music and light entertainment will enhance their sales and training events and association meetings. Most meeting planners book professional speakers and presenters for thousands of dollars. Why not book me for hundreds of dollars to create the perfectly hosted and musical venue? A blast of the theme song from the Rocky movies can really lift up a sales award banquet, etc.

For some corporate meeting clients, we do music trivia events, pre and post speaker introductions music, MC work, background music for awards, karaoke events, and break time music. Attendees at these group events loved the extra punch provided by my superior command of the right music for the right time. I was up to two business/corporate events a week and that allowed me to cut back to doing just four to six night events per month—a welcome break!

Companies pay better than wedding dances and the time commitment is shorter. The meeting planners are mostly interested in quality issues when it comes to these high pro-file events so they don't scoff at a few hundred bucks like the brides do. And not one corporate music gig goes by without it leading to at least one wedding event prospect.

This business still requires heavy "roadie" work. Setting up and tearing down of my music library and equipment gets tedious at times. Even with my ergonomically customized dolly, there is a lot of lifting of speakers and lights to set up and tear down the shows. I hired Marie's eighteen-year-old nephew to do part-time roadie support. He is a good, entertaining kid who would do this work for free just to be around this business. He has a band and doesn't want to go to college yet. His young back helped save mine!

I love being a "Musical Master of Ceremonies" and my business now, after two years, grosses about $125,000 per year. Marie runs the books and the scheduling from our modern home office. We all work hard, but we also have some great down time to just be with each other as a family. Some days we have no gigs at all so we focus on calling people or blogging around myspace.com to remind people we are available.

I hit LinkedIn.com to promote the business services side. I heavily use the status update box ("What are you working on?") because my near daily updates on that go out to and beyond my 600 people I am connected to. I often offer some music trivia question to keep my profile high.

I enjoy making people's lives more lively and enjoyable through music and entertainment. It took a lot of effort to get to the point we are now at. In retrospect, getting laid off wasn't so bad since I learned so much prior to being cut.

In a few years we may hang up our microphones and hire college kids to do the performances, but right now we are in a very good place. Getting dumped by a "steady employer" wasn't so bad after the shock subsided and we built on our strengths.

ૐ

To learn what websites were helpful to
Ronnie, please visit **www.growmedia.com**.

# 17

# Don't Sit On Your Assets

## Sales Rep Rex Rents His Database

Here is my journal of how I got started in my new endeavor. Use it as you see fit and I hope my story helps someone else out. I appreciate your encouragement during my career transition. I love this concept!

Thanks again,
Rex

**February 20:**

The merger of the two biggest companies in my product sector will probably kill my sales rep career in my market. After 16 years of being an independent manufacturer's representative in the durable medical equipment sector, I now fear a huge income decline. My three most profitable lines are being taken away. I can't pick up similar lines through other companies because the acquiring firm has bought out most of the competition. They will tightly regulate product distribution and market share.

They use *employee* sales reps on a base salary and pay them quarterly bonuses. If they actually do hire me, my compensation will go down by about half!

I put in over 35,000 miles of windshield time last year. My territory is over a thousand miles wide so I am always on the go. People think it is glamorous to host clients to golf, sports events, lunches, dinners, happy hours and such but it can get to be a grind after this many years. It can be especially nerve-wracking during an Illinois or Iowa blizzard.

The good news is these efforts have paid off nicely for me. I have built at least five hundred key relationships and friendships with doctors, therapists, hospital administrators, and purchasing agents. It has all worked out for me because I am a zealot about maintaining those relationships. I visit, see, call, email, poke, text and Twitter the friends in my turf on a regular basis. They know and trust me and I work hard at maintaining that. I know the names of their family members and most of the buyers' birthdays by memory.

I have loved being self-employed for most of my time in this industry. I learned at first by working for someone else before breaking out on my own. I love the independence and work for a great boss—me! The idea of looking for a job as an employee is downright depressing.

**March 20:**

It is bleak out there. Most viable product lines to rep for have been secured by some other rep or the manufacturer's *employee* salesperson. I see more of that these days—the manufacturers are hiring their own sales forces. If I were to try to get by on just selling my secondary lines in my territory, it wouldn't cover the price of gas. And I can't just dump the relationships I have built up!

The acquiring monopolist company has elected not to hire me. They went with someone who "is a closer match for our criteria." I think they know from experience how tough it is to convert a war-horse, independent like me into a company man who will work happily in their comp system. They'll hire some "snot nose" rookie who has a *two-year* track record of selling photocopiers!

Our liquid investments will allow me to pay my household bills for around six months, but I don't want to use that money for groceries and house payments. My wife Deb and I are restless because next month I will receive my LAST commission check from my former best line. *That* is a sinking feeling.

**April 7**

A career coach I chatted with helped me clarify my goals, needs and dreams. He helped me realize the career assets that I already do possess. I had a good idea of what my strengths and assets were, but he helped me clarify things well and put me on the right track.

A tool by The Gallup Organization is called the Strengths-Finder. It formally endorsed my top strengths that include: "Relator," someone with "WOO" and an "Input" guy.

These classifications verified why I like to deepen my relationships, win others over (WOO) in group or one-on-one settings, and that I am good at and like to collect data and information (Input). This all explained the successes I have had over the years in my business. The outcome of all that was my focus on my biggest asset: *Six Hundred Established Business Relationships.*

We discussed how typically a person's number one asset

is the thing that is "closest to money." So those strengths have helped me make the most money possible and enjoy doing so. My deep network of buyers in this region's medical community is unmatched. I felt like that career coach was more like a shrink who helped me uncover some cool stuff about me.

**May 20**

Things are taking shape. My hundreds of healthcare buyer relationships are now *"For Rent."* Instead of trying to find some*thing* to sell to these 600 people, I am going to "rent" *access to* these people.

My access to this group of doctors, nurses, therapists, secretaries, purchasing managers, VPs, hospital administrators, and CEOs is my most valuable asset. These people get hundreds of sales pitches every month so their collective attention is worth millions of dollars.

Hundreds of companies want to sell products and services to "my" buyers so, for a fee I will introduce *other* sales professionals to them. I will promote my "Introduction Services" at every medical conference, association meeting, and device or Durable Medical Equipment vendor show that I can get into. I will charge a flat fee, or an ongoing retainer, or earn a percentage of the profit made from the sales I help to occur. How I get paid will depend upon the product, service, and/or the involvement I have. The bottom line is that I will help my paying clients get in front of the buyers I have cultivated over all these years.

Only vendors who I respect and trust will be able to gain access to my community. My reputation means everything. For a creative finder's fee, I will help approved sellers act as an outsourced purchasing service of sorts.

My former buyers will rely on me to save them time and I will act as a screener of sorts for them. Only the best reps with the most strategic prices will get access to "my" buyers.

Some sellers may not be willing to give me a finder's fee from their earnings. But the smart ones will realize that paying me 5% of their proceeds from a sale is much better than no sale at all! We all know that it takes up to six months to crack open a new account. I can get my clients in front of my network in six *days*!

I laid out the content for a three-fold brochure in a couple of hours and my neighbor is a whiz-bang with graphics on her MAC Computer. She took my content, made it look great, and I emailed it to the nearby FedEx Office shop. *Including* the nice dinner I'll buy her and her husband, I have a professional looking, semi-glossy handout piece for $400 bucks!

I did my own web page via the templates on **www.enom.com**. For under $20 a month I have an acceptable brochure-like, three-page web site. It is truly basic but it does all I need it to do. My business is based on *human* relationships.

**August 20:**

Demand is high! The word in my region is out. I have several manufacturers interested in becoming my clients. I may not be able to keep up with all the transactions this might cause. I will limit the number of my paying clients to insure that I still maintain the high quality "filtering" that I am known for.

I think I need to charge *more* for this service. Some of the big name vendors who want to get into this region are classifying me as a Sales Consultant and are discussing generous retainers. It is completely worth it to them to cut their sales lead time from six months to six days.

I have *nine* vendor deals in the final stages and one has already begun paying me on a retainer basis. One of them has been trying to get into this territory for years and they have promised me a bonus of 1% of net profit on capitol equipment purchases that I help to broker.

&#x218b;

This concept has tremendous financial potential and I will have a lot less windshield time. My selling clients will do the on-site presentations and follow-ups, with an occasional "housekeeping" follow up call. All I do is introduce people after I am convinced the sellers are legit and their reps aren't jerks. And I check to be sure my community needs or is ready for a product as well. That way my vendors don't annoy my community.

I still get to golf and wine and dine my former buyers as much or as little as I want. Plus I get to *stay home* and work the phone and my social networks when winter blizzards hit!

It is fun and I am glad I figured out a way to build on the asset base I have.

&#x218b;

To learn what Internet resources were helpful to Rex, please go to **www.growmedia.com**

# 18

# Promote Yourself into Profits

## VP Leon Hypes Himself in a Former Niche

"Did you hear about Leon? He is one of the thirty who are getting laid off during this round of cuts! You'd think the legislative issues affecting our health insurance industry would make us hold onto an influential lobbyist like him! From what I hear, he's one of the best in the state. They say he's got solid relationships with most of the key state legislators in Phoenix.

I wonder what Leon is going to do—he makes big VP money and our city has a tight job market. He's a lawyer by training, but I heard he didn't want to practice in a firm. I guess he enjoys the lobbyist setting more than private practice or general counsel work. His son lives with Leon's ex-wife but starts on the high school basketball team, so Leon wouldn't want to relocate to some out of state job."

જી

"Did you hear about Leon? He has a whole new career.

My friend Susan from Finance lunched with him the other day and here's the scoop: Leon is now a professional consultant! His severance package was lame since he hadn't worked here very long.

He had little luck landing another corporate job so he postured himself as a short-term, independent consultant to companies. People *were* interested in him on a temporary, independent basis and he molded that into a consulting business. So, now he is just selling his knowledge.

I hear that people in our business like other vendors, customers, providers, and others are interested in hearing Leon's expertise and opinions about our industry. He earns up to $4,000 *per day* for a speaking or consulting gig at companies and association meetings! And it sounds like he has a handful of engagements a month. Susan said Leon's success is due to his tireless self-promotion and self-marketing.

The funny thing is that Leon never seemed to be a "sales type" of person. He was always busy pitching and persuading others to do things that were good for our company. Stuff like contacting our representatives about legislative bills in the state capital. He worked the "human network" like nobody's business.

He was always on the phone or emailing people. It seemed like that is all he did. I know...I worked on the same floor as Legal for awhile. I bet he made four dozen outside contacts every day as he worked to help this company, which ended up stabbing him in the back.

Susan also said Leon works inside the same network of people he built when he worked here. She said he has a compelling pitch that is unique to him and that it captivates potential prospects. It only lasts about thirty seconds and it is focused on the most compelling need of the prospect he is talking to. It *isn't* about *him*.

I guess Leon postures himself so potential customers think that they are *missing* key strategic information if they don't hire him. I saw his social media profile on the Internet and he even has a 1 minute video there and on YouTube. He's so handsome and articulate on those sites! He really sounds like an expert. He learned a lot when he worked here."

It sounds like he has made a great life for himself since getting dumped here 18 months ago. He's earning great money, gets to travel, hangs around with important people, gets recognition in the press and on related blogs, has a lot of independence and is very stimulated. So, I guess he's a great example of success, not that he wasn't successful when he worked here..."

"He was smart enough to find a tight but important industry niche in which he tirelessly promotes himself as an expert. He promotes himself on YouTube, LinkedIn, MySpace, Twitter, FaceBook, Wordpress.com and other social media. It isn't, I think, just *having* the skills and knowledge, it is just as important to promote oneself as the purveyor of that knowledge."

"But he really works hard. I heard that when he first started his business, he took a night job at a convenience store to help with his cash flow. After a nap, I guess he could work most of the day on his new venture. It tires me out to think about how hard he works.

Leon offered to buy me lunch next month to get my opinion on a key industry issue. He wants *MY* opinion so I will be happy to tell him what I know. He *is* single you know!"

ॐ

137

For web resources which were helpful to
Leon, please go to www.growmedia.com.

# 19

# Who Do You Know?

## Mainframe Mary Changes Hats at Her Former Employer

Her layoff wasn't particularly shocking. Each year Mary's financial services employer routinely cut 100 to 200 of their 4,000 person employees. There appeared to be an unwritten rule to purge "the bottom five percent" of the employees before the annual stockholder meeting in November. Everyone wondered who the "bottom five percent" was. Employees referred to the regular layoff event as "Black Thursday,."

Mary had been with the company for over ten years. She was a computer operations supervisor over a very specialized, small group that coordinated the Job Control Language functions of the IBM mainframe computers that ran hundreds of customer billing systems. At some companies, software developers did this type of work, but Mary's company had allowed a small team of people to evolve into its own little functional area. Mary worked her way into management of the team of 7 full-time people.

On this Black Thursday however her team was no longer hidden. The whole group got axed and the plan was to out-source the work to an underutilized programming team or possibly even offshore it.

Mary's severance package worked out to one month of pay for every year she had been employed with the company. To get this money she had to sign an agreement stating she would not sue the company for any reason including Age Discrimination, which had always been silently lurking around the corner, she felt.

She signed the contract because she knew the job market to be a harsh one. Not only was the biggest recession in thirty years raging, but her skills were extremely narrow; solid but narrow. Few other firms in the St. Louis area would have evolved the way her fast-growth employer had.

She'd worked her way into her last position after starting with the company as a data entry temp. She had no degree and worked her way up at the high growth firm because she was in the right place at the right time, and because she had excellent logic skills.

A computer operations job she'd earned morphed into the Job Control Language job where she eventually became the Team Lead after demonstrating her natural people skills. Her climb up the corporate ladder had been a true inside job.

ಎಲ

After taking a week off to get her mind around her layoff, Mary worked on her job hunt for at least six hours each day. Her resume was professionally prepared, her attire perfect, her attitude tops, and her drive strong.

But even with all that she didn't land even one interview

in the computer field. She tweaked her resume into several versions but that didn't change her hit ratio. She started leaving the 'salary history' and 'salary required' boxes blank when the online application would allow it. Also, she'd put "$1" or "$0" in those online fields when the system required a number in order for her to submit her application. She was depressed how robotic applying for a job had become.

Relocation was not an option due to a home improvement loan she and her husband had taken out. That note made them close to 'upside down' in their mortgage to be able to sell their home in a flat real estate market. She couldn't find any appropriate jobs in the region anyway.

By Easter, Mary was very discouraged. She'd sent out a total of 89 online or hardcopy resumes to any job that even looked *close* to what she could do. This activity led to four initial interviews, one final interview, and no job offers.

Mary was encouraged to apply for a job as a customer service representative at a teleservices firm where her neighbor was a manger. Normally Mary's online application would be rejected because she was "overqualified" but the neighbor assured Mary the application could be "walked through" which would lead to a certain job interview.

"So that is what the 'Hidden Job Market' is" Mary said to her husband Ray. He thought she should take the job even though it paid around half of what her former job did.

"A job is a job," he said, "and in the economy you maybe have to take whatever you can get." He sighed and went on. "We are already ditching the cell phones and the cutting the cable TV package to a bare minimum. We have to keep the Internet service so you can apply for jobs, and we have already benefited from eating out very little. And, your lazy brother said he'd buy this big screen TV from us for what we owe on it. We'll get by."

Ray was practical but his comments reminded Mary how the family had overreached their budget with too much debt. Her severance fund was fading fast and the family budget, complete with too much fat, had come to rely on her Soon-To-Vanish Income. They couldn't get by on Ray's income alone.

≥≥

After the first interview at her neighbor's company, it occurred to Mary there were similar positions at her former employer. In fact, there was a whole department of people doing this kind of work and Mary knew Jane, the supervisor of that area. Jane was the extroverted shortstop on one of the teams from the company's softball league. Time for lunch with Jane!

The day before lunch with Jane, it occurred to Mary that her former employer was still conducting its day-to-day business. They hadn't ground down to a halt without her help. There were still thousands of people there who WERE employed despite the negative headlines about the place.

Jane and Mary got all caught up at a trendy pasta restaurant. There was an Assistant Supervisor position coming available in the Customer Call-Back Department. This job reported to a friend of Jane's and Mary's background was perfect. She had technical skills, high attention to detail, supervisory experience, strong company knowledge, and a super personality. Jane spoke to her friend Michelle who granted Mary an interview.

Of concern to Michelle, was the job's lower pay grade than what Mary held in her old IT job. Mary assured Michelle that months of unemployment made any job with the company look great. She assured her potential new boss that she would *not* attempt to get other internal jobs for at least 2 years, if she were hired.

Mary's former supervisors provided stellar references and Michelle liked Mary's determination to prove herself in a new area. Despite some strong internal competition, Mary was offered the job at a 35% pay cut from her old job. Mary viewed this as a 65% increase over her "present" income of *zero*!

Mary started back with the firm and was a quick study. She kicked herself for taking so long to job hunt with the people she already knew. When she left, Mary's separation file said she was eligible for rehire, but at the time of her layoff her pride and anger had blocked her from even thinking about ever working there again. Now she was thrilled for the opportunity.

The new department was livelier than her old job and it wore her out to have so much people contact over the whole day. But Mary's extroverted ways and new exercise routine at the company wellness center helped her adapt.

Her family cut back on its spending now that they knew there is no 'sure thing' out there. The days of assuming there will always be a steady paycheck are long gone. They are running a tighter financial ship now and actually becoming closer as a family due to less technology in their lives.

An added perk for Mary's new job was how her previous vacation time and retirement accruals were reinstated since she was gone from the company for just under six months. Her deep pool of vacation time made her pay cut hurt less.

Mary has enrolled in two night classes at the local community college. She sees less of her family but doesn't miss hanging out and watching the small screen TV with Ray.

"A little less *American Idol* and a little more 'Business

Administration 101' will help me become more valuable to my employer," she told Jane. "I want to have a backup plan in place in case this ever happens to me again."

The anniversary of Mary's "Blackest Thursday" came and went. She happily kept her new job and mused that she *must now* be in the *top 95%!*

❧

For Internet resources helpful to
Mary, please see **www.growmedia.com**.

# 20

# Follow Your Heart

## Librarian Larry Learns to Sell Data

Paul,

I met this crazy guy the other day at a swap meet. He has a great story so we had some beers together and I interviewed the heck out of him. Here is what I learned:

ह♥

Larry's dad was a mechanic who loved cars. Larry's best memories of his dad were the times when they spent endless hours of tinkering on various vehicles in the garage of Larry's childhood home in Illinois. It fit for Larry to grow up and call himself "My Old Car Guy" because he could tell you make, model, and engine sizes of almost every American car made since the 1940s. He said he's bought, sold, owned, traded, built and parted out about 100 cars in his lifetime.

His dad told Larry to go into a field other than mechanic work as a career because Larry could always work on cars as a hobby. So Larry went to college but couldn't figure out a major. He was always drawn back to cars and that didn't really fit at the liberal arts college he attended. At college, Larry spent lots of time using the college's databases and powerful computers to do research. Unfortunately that research was mostly focused on cars.

When he reached the deadline of choosing a major, Larry selected Library Science. And you guessed why—so he could be close to and have access to research tools and databases. He figured a "white collar" job would please his father but still stay close to his own passion for the automotive industry.

Library Science was an unusual college major for a guy with grease under fingernails, but he said it was also a good way to meet women, the dominant gender in that field. One woman he met at the college library was Jessie. They fell in love and got married two weeks after their joint college graduation.

ঌ

Larry's first job after college was as a part-time librarian at a smaller county library system. The arrangement worked well since it gave him the flexibility to work on friends' cars at their homes. Usually he'd work on these projects for the companionship or beer and no money changed hands. Sometimes however, he'd accept bartered parts or cash, depending on how many hours he'd put in and how well he knew the person he'd do the work for.

Larry eventually moved into a full-time Librarian Assistant job at a suburban Chicago area library. The commute was long but the job represented better money and offered full-time benefits.

Three years later, Larry and Jessie had a baby daughter. While she took some time from his hobby, Larry's skill, connections and knowledge of classic and modern cars just kept growing. He kept working on cars and researching them too. During his off hours, he built his reputation as a connected guy who could find and appraise models and locate hard-to-find parts. He constantly found, swapped, bartered and introduced buyers and sellers in several automotive genres.

Larry wished he could quit his library job and pursue the passion that was starting to give him "guru status" in the classic auto world. His job's insurance benefits enslaved him to the world of being an employee even though he felt pretty sure he could make more money in the car world. Jessie made good income working part-time for a high rolling commercial real estate professional, but her job had no insurance benefits and the income was often sporadic.

Jessie had many friends she'd made inside of Larry's auto world but their now toddler daughter had a medical condition requiring expensive, ongoing treatments. It was mandatory to maintain good health insurance.

అ

An election year rolled around and the incumbent mayor proposed budget cuts to the library in response to grandstanding by his opponent. The adversary had said the mayor's "pet project" was the library system, and it was the reason a high profile crime in their suburb had "gone undeterred." Indirectly, the library had become an emotional, negative campaign issue.

After the election, Larry was identified as the last full-timer hired at his branch. Therefore he got a sixty-day termination notice. Severance packages were unheard of at his tenure and his level. He was a popular librarian due the steady stream of automotive seminars and speakers he'd regularly lined up to use the library's meeting room. Four car clubs were now holding regular meetings at Larry's library branch. Circulation and foot traffic were up significantly there and the branch's Director knew why.

The couple's daughter was now in school, and Jessie went to work full time for a fast-growing, online job posting board. The family was happy to see Jessie's employer offer health insurance. And she loved her new job. The company was growing fast despite the recession of the early 2000's. But the couple's new home had been purchased based on both of their incomes. And Larry wasn't pulling his share of the weight on that front.

Larry's automotive community provided six offers in auto parts stores, auto sales, and auto mechanics. But Larry was an "Input Guy" whose real desire was to build an "automotive information empire." He just needed to figure out how to monetize what he knew.

His best side income over the years was from fees he earned helping people find and buy hard to find parts or vehicles for buyers and sellers. That kind of activity represented the least amount of time for the most amount of profit.

Larry's research skills helped him utilize an emerging firm called eBay where he regularly found, sold, and resold parts to and from collectors who had plenty of cash to spend on their car hobbies, despite the recession. His early and heavy use of the site may have contributed to that online giant's formation of an entire division dedicated to auto-related sales.

Using that tool, and sometimes by just serving as the direct intermediary, Larry earned a finder's fee as he enabled a transaction. If he didn't know the person who might have the part of the car a buyer was seeking, he knew someone who knew that person. Since he never actually owned any of the parts or vehicles, he did not need a dealer's license. But he did form an official business entity.

Over the years, he had built a database of over 1,000 classic car related contacts. Due to his library science background, he'd organized that data to be able to access his information from a variety of different angles. He could instantly access and find vehicles, parts, vendors, suppliers, and people with his database. His finder's fee income grew but was still highly sporadic. It held more volatility than he could take since he didn't have a steady job.

Larry cultivated his contacts to do more restoration work on people's hot rods and classic cars. Many car buffs Larry knew didn't have time to get their own cars ready for shows and contests. Larry often found himself very busy preparing vehicles before major and minor car shows and contests in the area. But he knew that nice stream of income would only be strong in the spring and summer car show season.

ॐ

After meeting and visiting with a job coach at a car show, Larry decided to merchandise his talent. The coach quickly recognized Larry was a walking, talking encyclopedia of car trivia and that skill might be marketable in a media format. They chatted another time or two by phone and the strategy of Larry offering subscription newsletters was born.

He knew from his library days how the internet offered oceans of data on every subject for free. He also knew it was still in the Wild West phase of its growth and new rules, norms, and tools were being established every month. Most niche web sites were far from profitable. He knew there were auto repair shops, dentist offices, parts stores, doctors' offices, libraries, and dozens of other niches which would like to have his entertaining and nostalgic *hardcopy* magazine in their offices and reception areas.

Based on his library background, he knew advertising sales and subscription purchases would sell slower in a recession. In recessions, hobbyists and companies spent less on extras. But he'd also seen individuals spend $56,000 cash for a 1973 lime green, fully-restored Dodge Super Bee.

"There are still people with means who will and can pay for things they want even in a recession," he told Jessie. "Even in The Great Depression, there were elite clubs where people who still had some money would quietly dine and danced. See the movie 'Cinderella Man' for an example."

His Dewey-Decimal-System-Trained-Mind combined with a stronger than average knowledge Google Search Engine Optimization helped Larry know the importance of niche markets. His newsletter niches would cater to Hot Rod, Corvette, Nomad, Thunderbird, Mopar Muscle Cars, and Harley Davidson audiences specifically. There were advanced competitors of web sites, glossy magazines, and newsprint rags in all these genres, but Larry's niche audiences focused on the regional states of Wisconsin, Illinois, Indiana, Ohio and Michigan, *only*.

His personalized stories, reports on events, brokerage of parts and vehicles all contributed to his reputation. He handed out the newsletters for free at car events for a few months. Later he began offering them for a subscription.

Postage and paper costs forced him to get a line of credit against his house to get things rolling. Jessie had earned a promotion and a raise already and was cautiously supportive of her husband's venture. It showed promise based on all the positive feedback the couple had received. She liked how his income was diversified via his restoration work, deal brokerage and now the emerging newsletters.

Larry also developed hilarious automotive-related talks which he gave at auto shows and swap meets, and even at some corporate events. Many guys who were into the classic car scene were sales executives at area corporations. Three of them had invited Larry into their sales training events because they knew their car friend had a good handle on how to grab people's emotions. Larry knew how to capture and peddle nostalgia and these sales managers wanted their sales staffs to learn from this. But Larry would be the last person to admit he knew anything about sales. As a Subject Matter Expert in the classic car world he knew a lot. And his passion for that topic captured the emotions of lots of people who had money to spend.

Two national level aftermarket parts vendors hired Larry to speak at their conferences and trade shows as well. They paid Larry an average of $1,000 each for his four talks which averaged about 90 minutes each. They also allowed him to pitch his newsletters and he gave new subscribers from those companies a preferred rate.

Larry's web site is really only a tool to enable him to pitch his newsletters and to allow people to sign up and pay online. He does offer an online delivery of the newsletters to people who subscribe to the hardcopy version. But that's an add-on only. He thinks *"The Polishing Rag"* needs to stay tangible and an extension of himself. It also drove emails and phone calls for the restoration and brokerage parts of his practice.

"Car guys are hands-on guys. They don't want to sit in front of computers all day. And also, I need hardcopy to hand out at all events I attend."

His web site is not a swap meet for buying and selling cars—there were other web sites that did that. Instead, he works with people he meets personally to help them locate their perfect vehicle or even parts. He is more like a personal matchmaker or headhunter.

He has over 1,000 subscribers in just over a year. He limits the number of ads and the number of pages per issue. That limits the amount of supply and demand per issue so he can charge premium rates. In the car business a low number of models produced increases the collector price. He says his ad space follows the same principal.

The thousands of libraries across the country are natural target customers for Larry's newsmagazine subscriptions. He knows how libraries work and feels he'll sell subscriptions to nearly every public library within two years. His *"Click and Clack"* style of information delivery is growing in popularity not only in libraries and car repair shops everywhere but he, as planned, is selling newsletters to doctor and dentist offices too. "Anywhere you see *Road and Track*, you will hopefully see my rag too," Larry was often heard to say.

Larry and his relatives have helped build his online visibility via a network of nearly 2,000 friends and connections on Facebook, Twitter followers and LinkedIn. He uses Event Inviters on those sites to make sure he keeps his groups aware of the auto-related events he is attending. His WordPress blog is another tool which he uses to raise his online visibility. He adds short blog entries there every Sunday night when his customers are dreading Monday mornings. He is careful to steer blog traffic back to his web site which sells subscriptions.

Jessie's large family helps produce and physically create and mail the letters out of the family's basement which now looks like a print and production shop. Jessie's cousin is a journalism major who helps out with some of the blog and newsletter writing. She takes all her guidance from Larry the input guy, though and his personality and knowledge is stamped all over his emerging automotive empire! He really turned his passion into a lifestyle.

৵

For Internet resources which were helpful to Larry, please see **www.growmedia.com**.

# 21

# Serving Differently

## Nurse Nancy Moves Out of Healthcare

Thanks for asking about the story of my career transition. It is all really based on my love of kids. I grew up in a large family and together with my husband Alvin we have 5 of our own kids too. Even in high school, I knew that I wanted to be a pediatric nurse so I pursued that profession with a passion. Upon graduation, I took a job at the large children's hospital in our city.

Working there mended and broke my heart each day. I can't describe how useful I feel when I provide comfort and healing to an ill child and his or her parents. But, there is the other side of that too. There are some patients who we couldn't help enough. That broke my heart each and every time we lost a patient.

Over the years, I worked into a part-time role at the hospital. That was helpful since my kids, all under the age of 12 at the time, were very busy. Alvin's career and pay were moving ahead nicely so my part-time pay was a nice contribution to the family budget, but not mandatory for us to get by. We are very involved in our kids' church and sports events so it was nice to work part time.

Last winter, the unimaginable happened. Alvin was laid off from his high-tech employer. He was not alone—dozens of others got the axe that day too. Due to his company's financial problems relating to what they call "The Dot Com Meltdown," he got very little severance upon separation.

I immediately bounced into a full-time work schedule and even added hours beyond that in order to earn overtime pay. Alvin took over the domestic front while he looked for work. His unemployment lasted over three months. Even though his JAVA programming talent is a high-demand skill, the tough economy prolonged his search.

After Alvin's paychecks resumed, I wanted to go back to part-time work again. Since the hospital was experiencing shortages of staff and liked my work, they pressured me to stay full time. That made me doubt if they were as employee-centered as they bragged about being. Plus, they were paying new nurses big sign-on bonuses but wouldn't pay those bonuses to the existing staff. I thought that was unfair.

Since we had moved to a suburb right before Alvin lost his job, the hospital job represented nearly an hour commute for me. I thought about finding a job at the pediatrician's office near our neighborhood. The whole big picture made me reconsider my occupational calling. My own family was first in my book—even above my patients. I started brainstorming. I once read *"When you are ready for a thing, it will appear."* I kept waiting for that revelation and telling everyone I was ready.

That month, our associate pastor asked me to substitute

for a youth group volunteer who had to pull out of an upcoming weekend youth retreat. My oldest was scheduled to go on that trip so I happily agreed. The event included the pastor, six other adults, and forty-five middle school kids!

The pastor asked me to lead one of the class sessions. I declined because I wasn't qualified. But, the pastor gently pressed me to try anyway. I did it and received good response from the kids and the adults who saw me. It was fun!

᪥

A month after that retreat, the pastor asked me to go to lunch with him and the senior pastor. At my favorite restaurant, they explained to me that our church's rapid growth demanded more paid staff. The full-time youth and education director needed to focus on youth only, so we needed to add a full-time parish education coordinator. They wanted ME to think and pray about considering that Parish Education Director position.

The position would pay for thirty-two hours per week. This would mean a few more hours of work per week at significantly less pay than I was used to. The job involved organizing, leading, managing, recruiting for, and teaching some of the many educational ministries at our church.

After a lot of prayer and talk with my family and friends, I agreed to go through the church's formal interview process. In the end, I was thrilled to be called to the position. There were other, better-trained candidates who had applied, but I got the job due to the church's comfort level with me. I felt very alive and excited to start this new ministry. The lower pay didn't seem to matter as Alvin's new job was going well.

I work more than thirty-two hours per week, and my kids are involved in many of the programs I teach or lead. I feel my work is a good example for them. The church is just two miles from home, so I enjoy flexibility with my work and home schedule. The staff is wonderful and the work is very rewarding. Being part of the faith journey for students of all ages is very enriching.

I now enjoy a strong sense of calling, and my family appears to be handling the transition quite well. My youngest now sees me more than ever because I can often bring him along to work.

Alvin's career interruption knocked me out of a comfortable routine which in turn showed me what I *didn't* want to do. I didn't want to work for my former large, corporate employer. Even though we were saving lives and working with children, it just wasn't what I wanted to do anymore because of the setting.

Years ago I would have never dreamed of going to work in a parish setting. I was a medical professional who was excellent at her work. I improved the world one patient at a time. I wasn't some administrator/teacher type! And the most amazing thing of all was that the church pursued and wanted me to join them!

I had no training or formal education in matters of religion or theology, and here I am heading up programs which guide hundreds through that process! Good thing I coordinate, rather than teach all that stuff! All my volunteer work at the church over the years really put me on this path for service to God. And I *do* feel called to do this!

My advice to others in career transition is to "look beyond the weeds" as they say. Try to not label yourself as one thing or another but look more at Your Core Passions. There were RNs I worked with who spent years specializing in one area of nursing. They couldn't see themselves working in a different specialty of nursing even though another area was still nursing! I say take the leap! Climb up to the top of the hill, look around, and see what other path you might go down. I am so thankful that I did! I was ready for a thing, and it appeared!

ം

To learn what Internet resources were helpful
to Nancy, see **www.growmedia.com.**

# 22

# Know and Work Your Niche

## School Principal Paula Plans Parties for Profit

**To: Event Planner**

**From: Principal Planning by Paula**

**RE: Your upcoming retirement party for Principal Adams**

Your retirement sendoff for Principal Adams at the end of this school year will, I'm sure, be a very special event. Perhaps my services can make it even more special for Mr. Adams and for the staff of his building.

*As founder of* <u>*Principal Planning by Paula,*</u> *I create & host parties & reunions that see their organizers relax & cause attendees to rave about the event for months.*

My status as a former top education professional in our community prods me to "test" people and groups who are hosting special events in the near future. Will your event for Mr. Adams pass the following quiz?

1. The best reason to consider use of my professional planning services for this event is:
    a. We don't know what our budget will be for the event.
    b. We are all very close to Principal Adams and this event will be very emotional.
    c. All of those who are planning the event are active, busy professionals.
    d. All of the above
2. Which of the following is most true?
    a. A professional event planner has the professional connections to enhance your party's content.
    b. Principal Planning by Paula has planned and executed dozens of quality events similar to what your group will host.
    c. Principal Planning by Paula has planned and executed eight retirement events for education professionals and has stellar references for each.
    d. All of the above.
3. How can *Principal Planning by Paula* save you money on this event and still insure a high-quality occasion?
    a. Paula's suppliers and vendors compete with one another so her prices are lower than you can get on your own.
    b. Paula's supply network can often deepen the discount even more for "non-profit" events such as yours.
    c. Paula's incredible event PR and sign up processes can drive high percentage of advanced registration which assures a bigger budget to create an even *more* memorable event.
    d. All of the above.

Of course the answer to each of the questions is "D - All of The Above." To back this "quiz" up, I have reprinted, with permission, the following unsolicited testimonial for my work:

> *Dear Paula,*
>
> *I want to express my deepest gratitude to you for what you did for my retirement event. While your visibility at the party was basically zero, I felt your presence in every detail. The food was fantastic, the atmosphere amazing, and the speakers were stupendous. I have known those speakers for decades, but your direction allowed their presentations to bring steady laughter and tears from the audience and me. I know this is true because they told me how well you prepared them for the event.*
>
> *Thanks so much for everything. Your event summarized my career perfectly and the memories from that evening will last a lifetime.*
>
> *Thanks again, Superintendent Johnson*

In review, the quiz and the testimonial speak for themselves. I'd be happy to visit with you regarding some particulars and specifics of an event like this. What too many people don't know is that my planning skills can often save people more money than what my fee is. Therefore people get a lot of extras they might not otherwise have, nearly for free!

My initial consultation with you regarding your upcoming event is free. I'd be honored to meet with you in person, by phone, by Tweet, or any of the major social networks I am on. If, after our meeting, your group decides not to use my services, you'll *still* receive my free booklet entitled, "Principal Planner Paula's Pointers for a Perfect Party.

Best wishes,
Paula Smith
Founder, Principal Planning by Paula

ॐ

Paul,

I have built a niche based on my "insider knowledge" of the educational community. I go after retiring educator events at area schools and colleges because I know that space. My hundreds of relationships formed after 30 years in local, public education created lots of friends and many opportunities to help school staffs to create memorable events.

I rely heavily on LinkedIn, MySpace, Twitter and FaceBook to stay in touch with all my friends and acquaintances in dozens of school buildings across the educational community. As you can see, I incorporated the TwitterVator Speech you helped me build into the heading of my introductory letter. It works!

This all helps me to nurture and keep in touch with my dozens of "lookouts" or "spies" I have at the facilities across the metro area. It is fun to keep in touch with everyone and they keep feeding me solid leads on retirement and other kinds of parties. There are so many Baby Boomers retiring these days—I am keeping busy!

Educator retirements did launch my planning/event business, but those types of events represent only about 40% of my revenues now. You see, teachers, principals, administrators, professors, and deans etc. almost all *have families*. And families have events including family reunions, weddings, baptisms, bar mitzvahs, retirement parties, 50th wedding anniversaries, 80th and 90th birthday parties; funerals, etc. etc. Success breeds referrals and I have developed a positive reputation in a fairly short time. That is due to two things: My constant self promotion and networking plus my flawless, obsessive-compulsive attention to event details! Networking at these family-related events has opened the door to me for corporate type of events too. But, I am almost too busy these days as is. I don't think I really want to add employees but I do use temp agencies for staff when I do some big events. That way I have the help when I need it but I don't have to keep paying someone's payroll in a slower time. I like to stay close to and hands-on with all of my events so I can control everything.

ॐ

People ask me how I got into this. As a single parent I had no room for any messing around when it came to my household budget. Even though my pay as a principal was pretty good, I worked a million hours. When I reached 27 years with the district I did the superintendent a favor and agreed to take on one building for him which nobody wanted to be principal of. That assignment was my hardest three years of my professional life, but I grew a lot as a professional at that building.

The main benefit of that assignment was it allowed me to negotiate an entire summer off between my old school assignment and my new one. Sure I did the recruiting of staff and a few summer meetings, but I also got to work very hard on planning my business.

As a school administrator you are already a planner of

schedules, events, manpower, budgets, processes and procedures. Doing event planning was old hat therefore, especially since I am known as a tough negotiator and a detail fanatic.

Well, that summer was my launching pad. I got the infrastructure in place and the ball slowly rolling on my new enterprise. I was *far* from being ready cash-flow wise, from quitting my day job. It took over two years of long hours as a principal and more hours as a planner wannabe before I was ready to start full-time at this.

ॐ

Now I have total flexibility and control of my career. I am thrilled I spent decades in the education world. I served lots of kids and teachers, *and* it positioned me for the success I now have. I really don't miss the naughty kids, the few teachers who are whiners, the small percentage of bad parents, and the unrealistic school board amateurs.

People tell me I have high energy and passion for this business. They are right because I love what I am doing. The bad economy hasn't even slowed me down because as you saw in my introductory letter, I SAVE people money on the events which they are going to have anyway.

I am *now* creating new kinds of memories for people and I love it!

Best Regards,
Paula Smith

ॐ

For web-based resources which were helpful
to Paula, please visit **www.growmedia.com**

# 23

# Build On Your Strengths

## Pastor Pete Motivates Corporate Congregations

Thanks for requesting to hear my story of career transition. Moving from my former career to my present occupation has not been easy, so perhaps my personal tale has some nuggets which will help your constituents.

My career transition started five years ago, after serving for 23 years as a parish pastor in a Protestant denomination. My last call of service was at a multi-staff, medium-sized church in a Pennsylvania community of less than 100,000 people.

I'd been at that church for eight years and we were doing good work. The congregation was comprised of many young families. I worked long hours and we had steady growth and things were sailing along.

One group of very vocal members had emerged, though. They were very adamant about a theological issue as it related to our national church body's social statement. The short version is that our congregation ended up splitting over this issue. Despite my decades of work as a shepherd and a mediator, I couldn't resolve the philosophical and emotional split which emerged between my congregation's more traditional verses the more progressive members. I worked too hard to keep the peace and alienated too many who were coming into power. Eventually I had no calling or job.

About that time, my wife Lisa had developed a nice career in the psychology department at the regional medical center. Because she was just realizing some of her potential there, and because she spent over two decades chasing my career from parish to parish, we chose to do our best to stay put in our present city. We loved the community and our home.

However, one can't live on love and Lisa's salary alone didn't pay all the bills. The church gave me six months of pay upon my departure as long as I promised to take my church membership somewhere else. Accepting that deal was a no-brainer!

As I pondered my future with no small amount of panic, I recalled how many times people told me they loved my sermons and preaching. I was often invited to speak at other congregations and church-wide regional and even national events and workshops.

Congregants often asked me for printouts or recordings of my sermons. Because of this my last two churches got equipped to make recordings of my sermons and they were made very available for free. At my last church, a local radio station carried our Sunday services. They often stated how their listeners routinely complimented and said that was why they tuned in.

So I had a big head when it came to my presentation ability. I developed the wild idea of becoming a paid, professional speaker. I fervently researched the concept and uncovered a hoard of data on the topic.

For years my work in the ministry had witnessed adversity in people's lives. I have seen all possible views of how people respond to crisis in their lives. Hundreds of counseling sessions with parishioners due to divorce, abuse, infidelity, disease, psychological problems, family or teenager issues, shocking or slow deaths—I have seen it all. Each person has a story and each one changed me. A recurring theme I witnessed over the years was how, with God's help, people *can* be highly resilient.

Becoming a professional speaker would be easy I thought, because I would simply perfect my message and take it on the road. I wouldn't have to create a new message each week for the same captive audience like I did at the congregation. I would be a roving soothsayer of advice and travel was not a problem.

I attended two workshops by professional speakers who specialize in helping people get into that business. They were expensive but worth it as those pros literally cut years from my learning curve. I read a dozen books, many articles, and listened to records of many professional speakers and consultants.

After weeks of input, I began to craft my own "signature theme." I learned I needed to offer my content in one-hour, half day, day-long, and even a weekend-long retreat version. I made demo recordings, built a web site off a template package and it only cost me $20 a month through a prominent hosting company. I was ready to go live with the web site which even had sample Podcasts and a YouTube type of demo or sample of my presentation. I was all set for clients and buyers to beat a path to my door. Then a strange thing happened: *Silence.*

What I learned over the next year is that a professional speaker needs a great presence, a good web site, strong demo recordings/videos, a timely topic and superior platforms skills. But, what he needs *most* of all is steady, constant self-promotion.

At first I hated the fact I had to sell myself. After all, I was a senior minister who possessed a quarter of century of unique experience, not to mention a superior "real world" message, plus I had a skilled, proven delivery of that message. Hundreds of people loved my content and they told me this all the time.

To keep some income coming into the home I had been doing steady pulpit supply or "temping" for vacationing pastors in the region. It wasn't enough. Lisa and I elected to liquidate one of our investments so I could continue to pursue my expensive "hobby." Without Lisa's support and belief, I would now be selling used cars instead of inspiration.

I went back and studied the top pros in the National Speakers Association. I bought more resources, practiced, and watched, this time with an eye for self promotion. A theologically trained shepherd of a non-profit organization typically has no training on self promotion. I missed that course in seminary!

At another speaker workshop where we were discussing self-promotion and marketing, I realized that I had definitely been a strong promoter in my previous career. I was a master at persuading people. I worked to persuade them to send their kids to Sunday School and Confirmation classes. I'd persuaded people to volunteer for the myriad of jobs it takes to run a worship service complete with music and Holy Communion. I persuaded people to run and teach in extensive educational and youth ministry operations. I'd persuaded people to seek counseling, to serve on committees and to teach and volunteer with other parish activities. I *was* a sales guy—a persuader for God's work. I realized how selling is simply telling a persuasive story and then persistently following up. I had been a mission pastor who started two congregations from scratch, so I did have those skills in sales. For some reason I didn't even realize that. Zig Ziglar once said that Jesus himself was a great salesman because when people threw objections to Him, He simply played the part of a salesman and asked a question or told a story!

ॐ

I immediately made a mental transfer and enthusiastically began marketing *myself* with a vengeance. I believed in my message and my value so I felt liberated to peddle myself like never before. I started doing free newsletter articles, talk radio shows, leave-behind brochures, hundreds of personal networking telephone calls and emails galore. The whole Social Media/Social Networking thing on the Internet was empowering too. At little to no cost, I could put my profile out on cyberspace via Linkedin, FaceBook, MySpace, Twitter, do a blog on WordPress.com and create several interest groups and sites to network with people.

But even with all the profiles on the web, the key I have learned is I still have to follow up with *people*. It is fine to make an impression on someone but rarely will they "buy" due to a positive impression alone. I need to build and keep the relationship moving forward. Even if it is a virtual "pen pal" type of relationship I need to be and stay proactive. I have to do this just like I did when I was trying to get new members to join my mission churches.

I even promoted my speaking services through local churches where I have strong relationships to springboard from. But I have to be pedantic in my follow-through because people get tons of noise these days.

I have been a substitute preacher in many area churches. Often those run a little bio on me so the parishioners know who is running their service. Of course I have my speaking services faintly worked into that paragraph. Four executives who attend those services have approached with inquiries about corporate work for them!

I gave free mini-talks to every group or service club within sixty miles of our community. I focused on selling myself at least two thirds of the time or more. And it slowly worked! My promotional efforts finally started paying off. I followed my mentors to the letter and ended up being somewhat in-demand on the topic of holistic health, and how to win in life by focusing on that. I water down the "God Stuff" when presenting workshops for corporations and have positioned myself as a "God Moved My Cheese" kind of speaker when appropriate. I help my clients help their employees or group's members handle the incredible pace of change in the world.

Being postured as a "business-savvy" clergy person was also an attention-getter with meeting planners and corporate human resources people. The suffering economy actually helped me get more gigs because I address the human condition. I am pleased to have something helpful to offer to so many.

I wrote a fifty-page booklet on my theme. It has no fancy binding or cover but I sell many copies through my PayPal account on my web site and they especially sell well out of the back of the room after my presentations. Being it is that long I was able to get an ISBN "number" for it from Bowker. I have it selling in a Print-On-Demand basis on Amazon. com (using their **www.createspace.com** service) and many other online bookstores. It is a great credibility builder and a good profit center. It only took me a month to collate my stories about how people have the spirit in them to come out on top. Thank goodness Lisa's sister in law is a good editor!

When I use real-life stories of people who have suffered and still come out on top, my audiences respond well. Everyone knows someone who has struggled or perhaps they struggled themselves. I often speak for free to various charitable groups and still do fine financially because my tearful audiences buy my products afterward.

அ

It took time for me to adjust to the fact I shouldn't just give away my written and recorded products. But, I have come to terms with selling my information. I believe now that if my audiences support me, I am able to *continue to afford to be "out there"* to support them and help *them* grow. And perceived value is critical. If people get a freebie, they don't value it. If they pay for it, they hold on to the information, use it again and again because they value it.

Often after my speeches, people ask me to follow up with a visit to problem areas at their companies or non-profit organizations. I am not a business-trained person but most of the problems in companies that I see stem from people not listening to each other. And, after building three large church facilities with volunteer services over the years, I know how to get people to communicate on the same page. And now I get paid to do this!

The bottom line is that by using all of the tools I just

mentioned, I have managed to double my top pastoral income after two years of work as a professional speaker, trainer and seminar leader. I earn between one and three thousand dollars for most presentations, sell a respectable amount of recorded and printed products, and even get paid a few dollars for helping clients listen to each other. There have been several dry spells, but I stay fairly busy and we run a very fiscally conservative household budget. With Lisa's steady job, we seem to be money ahead 90% of the time.

This didn't happen overnight—we nearly had to move out of our home toward the end of my first year in this crazy business. But, it has been a wonderful second career for me. My foundation for success is strictly based on what I learned during my first career as a parish pastor. I loved that work and I also love this work. And I give thanks to God for the resourcefulness of the human soul.

æ

Websites which were helpful to Pastor Pete can be found at **www.growmedia.com**.

# 24

# Simplify Your Salary Needs

## Researcher Rick Burns Up the Slopes

Paul,

Last week when I was at Aspen I met a guy you'd be interested in hearing about. He has a pretty cool life. We were doing the small-talk routine while going up a chair lift. When he told me about his interesting background, I offered to buy him lunch since I knew you would want me to learn all about his life. You owe me $59.54 for lunch (yes, we had a few drinks)!

Dave

ॐ

Rick is originally from New York City but has lived in Aspen, Colorado for almost 3 years now. He is a cyber ski bum.

He grew up near ski country in Vermont and graduated from an Ivy League school. He compliantly landed a job in Lower Manhattan utilizing his two majors of economics and public relations. It was an entry-level job in the investor relations department of a huge chemical company.

He flourished in that department because he liked the action. The public relations department handled the news media most of the time, but Rick's Investor Relations group typically kept the mid-level investors informed. The top investors went to the C-Levels for their feedback but Rick's group fed data to the lower-to-mid-sized institutional investors and fund managers.

After Rick's first year at the firm, the company suffered a crisis regarding the rumored toxicity of one of its general use products. In the hour the story broke, one major institutional investor could not reach his normal C-level contact or that guy's administrative assistant. Impatient, the fund manager called the Investor Relations Department and ended up talking to Rick who was eating lunch at his desk.

Even with no details about the crisis, Rick was great on his feet. He calmed the very concerned heavy hitter on the other end of the phone. Rick provided a very general response but it was done in a way that his analysis pacified the investor, who ended up *not* selling his large position in the firm. A senior official at that fund later told Rick's boss how the greenhorn's real-time feedback and strategic talking points helped calm everyone down.

Rick didn't single-handedly keep that fund from dumping its holdings, but he certainly did help to save the day. He earned a nice bonus and hung on to work in the department for three more years. He eventually earned the title of Assistant Manager of the Investor Relations department.

That group had low turnover, and other jobs in the company were just not opening up. Rick had earned a golden boy status yet he couldn't seem to capitalize on it. It made him susceptible to a head-hunter's call who encouraged Rick to get on the dot-com band wagon.

In a new position with a dot-com start-up firm, Rick was promised the title of department director and would have thousands of free stock options. Rick scrutinized the backing of the firm in great detail. Investor support by smart people was plentiful, and the business model actually seemed like it could become profitable. Projections were very rosy. He took the job and quickly built a top-notch investor relations department for the small company.

⊱

After almost two years and three rounds of investor financing one of the key investors died suddenly. This prompted the other investors to back out. Now Rick's employer looked like too many other dot-com companies which were under-funded and overextended.

The only thing that could save the firm was another shot of $10 Million, and Rick knew that wouldn't happen in the post-Y2K, Post 9-11 climate. Rick and his co-workers were suddenly out of jobs and used their stock option contracts for dart board practice.

Rick decided to use what was left of his savings to go skiing in Colorado and ponder his future. Nobody was hiring in the New England area so he figured a road trip would be just as helpful as tilting at windmills that had "NOT Hiring" signs in their windows. He had been a hero in a huge corporation and a key man in a crashed-and-burned start-up that never really got started. He felt lost.

On the chair lift at Aspen he met a self-employed management consultant who detailed the pros and cons of his own business. This man earned a good living and seemed to have a nice sense of control over his life. Rick decided that this is what he wanted to do for his next career. But at the ripe young age 28 he wasn't sure what kind of consultant to try to become.

Rick was more of an analytical than he was a salesman or rainmaker kind of person. His chair lift counselor had said a consultant has to continually promote himself until he is thought of as the "go to" guy. His mentor warned how most consultants have serious "income valleys" for their first two or three years in business—especially during a recession.

So Rick had to figure out how to peddle what he knew without being a spammer or telemarketer. He determined his Unique Selling Proposition was his ability to find, obtain, package, and deliver strategic, investment-related research.

This wasn't about picking stocks or being a broker or a even a Wall Street Analyst type. Instead, he wanted to be more of a "private detective" of information about companies which were making strategic moves. If Rick's potential clients wanted to know about a specific product direction of a competitor, Rick could be paid to get that kind of answer.

He planned to find information which firms wouldn't or couldn't get on their own. He told me he doesn't do any hacking, illicit espionage or illegal, dark stuff. Rather, he is gifted at getting public information over the Net, from libraries, and from chatty current and former employees. He is amazed at what someone can learn from online resumes alone! Rick is also intrigued how companies spend millions of dollars to protect themselves with antivirus software and firewalls only to go on to see their very own employees talk too much in press releases, job interviews, and blogs.

After the ski lifts closed we met up again so he could show me his set up. I don't know why he trusted me—it might have been the three beers I bought him over our long lunch or the fact I am well connected in New York. He lives and works out of a 500 square-foot space above a bar. It isn't really living space and doesn't have a bathroom. His pad costs him only $500 a month because it isn't actually inhabitable according to the fire marshal.

"The fire marshal would shit if he knew I had a hotplate up here."

The room was a semi-finished attic and Rick had convinced a college friend who manages the bar to let him hang out there. He has a small fridge, a microwave, a hot plate, three pieces of cookware and he borrows silverware from the bar. He has one of those fancy air mattresses for a bed and stacks his sportswear and casual clothing (he donated all of his suits to Goodwill) in some wooden boxes.

"I don't entertain much," he explained when the look on my face told him I thought he led a Spartan lifestyle. "But I do ski and ride lot!"

Jamal is a ski bum buddy of Rick's who manages the front desk at a close-by health spa and fitness club. He lets Rick use that facility's shower room.

"I've also picked up seven new clients in the health club—the sauna is a great place to start conversations with visiting businessmen."

કે

He *is* a real cybersleuth—a kind of private detective of the Internet. He sells himself as an Online Strategic Research specialist. He doesn't have his own web site but instead describes his services on the big social networking sites. And he keeps the descriptions of his services very vague on those sites.

"Because those profiles are free," is what he told me when I asked why he has no web site of his own. "Most of my clients come from chair lifts, saunas and word of mouth. I hardly even need a profile on those social networking sites. Mine is a 'quiet' business." He explained how he did hire a job coach type of person to help him build his profile for him.

"He really knew how to discretely portray the work I do so it was $500 well spent." He also uses strategic blogging and chatting on investor relations message boards to build awareness of his services in a very discrete and casual way.

He is a master of marketing but he is not a sales kind of guy—he's really an introvert.

On the ski lift he'll smoothly *start* casual conversations like he did with me. He starts his low key inquiry of "Where are you from?"

From there he moves into "What do you do there?" Sometimes prospects ask him where *he* is from and after he tells them,

"Here." Then they *always* say,

"That must be nice and he can see them thinking, *How does a young guy like you afford to live here?*" He waits with a pregnant pause and they usually ask how he does afford to live in Aspen.

That conversation flow has led to 29 client engagements in two years! He has turned the "Elevator Speech" into a "Chair Lift" Speech!

I don't know why he'd lie to me about his average number of projects a month. He says he does three. Some projects take forty or fifty hours of research and writing and others only require ten or fifteen hours. He said the average project takes about 20 hours and his average project/report fee is around $2,500. The fee is typically based on billable hours like a lawyer. He is now turning down work but might subcontract some out to one of his college buddies.

Rick's only expenses are his cheap rent, his season pass lift ticket, a *little* food (since so many people buy him lunch and dinner—including me!), his hefty student loan payment, his top-of-the-line computer equipment, his report paper and binders and packaging materials. He also buys five paid online business database subscription services, and has a Blackberry *and* an iPhone. He gets free hi-speed Wi-Fi Internet service from the bar below him and he doesn't even own a vehicle. I scoffed at him not having a car and he said, "Where do I need to go? I have no commute and I live where people *come* to vacation. Parking my high-end mountain bike is free!"

I told him he should rent an office in a nearby non-skiing town, hire a sales and research staff and maybe he could eventually sell his strategic boutique business for a really nice chunk of change. His answer taught me a life lesson: "Dude! That would be too much hassle." He explained how building his business to the point where it would be sellable would take *at least* four years of long days and high stress. Then *if* he could sell it, he wondered mockingly what he would then do with himself.

"If I had a cool million in the bank then I would be able to do what—ski and mountain bike all day? Don't you get it...I do that *now*!"

❧

For web sites which Rick relies upon,
please see www.growmedia.com.

181

# 25

# Use Your Connections

## Sales Rep Vicki Wades Into Venture Capital

My college major was sales and marketing because I have been a persuasive person all of my life. I sold more Girl Scout cookies than anyone in my suburb and the big tip money I earned from my paper routes and waitress jobs gave me a "tax problem" while I was still a teenager. Mom is the real extrovert, so I "blame" her for my outgoing nature.

My first post-college job was selling for a health-care products company. My customers were clinics, doctor's offices, and hospitals. After just two years, I became the best producer company-wide for our regional firm.

I declined a promotion to sales manager as I didn't want to baby sit unmotivated peers, fill out reports for half the day in a cubicle, nor was I interested in a pay cut. I was born to manage and build my *own* territory. I made nearly $124,000 in year three. Not bad money for that "blabbermouth girl from the suburbs!"

Then Dad's prediction came true. He had said that often when sales reps get too successful, they end up getting their territory cut in half or a third. Their employers think that since the rep is so good, she can "spin her magic" in a new, underperforming territory again and again.

My employer must have heard my dad discuss this because in year three of my rocking employment, they pulled three of my key accounts away and gave them to other marginal producers at our company! They told me I had the skills needed to turn marginal clients into main ones and that I could go find new major clients in my new region. And they said those new clients would replace my former commissions! Not! For a mid market sales-driven company, they were sure stupid about sales!

The fact was that I had made those customers into key accounts! I hunted and farmed all of the relationships at those companies—dozens and dozens of them. I had turned those clients into the cherry accounts they now were. Now they want to hand my trophies over to a marginal rep or a new male rep that had done nothing to earn it? Give me a break!

Because I had $27,000 in liquid savings and investments, I was pissed off enough to quit on the spot. I had no idea what I was going to do next but I was furious. They begged me to come back but my pride was hurt. I had busted my butt to get to that point and I was darn good at my job. Since they had shown that side of themselves to me, I felt like I had outgrown their good-old-boy company.

A few of my college friends had gotten involved in the early 2000's with the dotcom, ecommerce buzz. Most of those fell flat on their head by 2002, but there were a few online related companies that had caught my interest.

California was still full of entrepreneurs and not every company went out of business in the famous dot com bust. I worked the online job boards, the social networks and my personal networks, eventually finding a job with a firm that planned to revolutionize the travel industry with a combination of travel bargains, travel-related advertising and travel planning. It was focused on being an ecommerce-only venture. They told me we had high-powered angels who invested "millions." I also heard that "venture capital firms were knocking at our door to hand us more money, despite the downturn." It all sounded very exciting and I accepted an offer that included thousands of stock options.

∂♥

My job would be to sell B2B travel-related services to the C-level executives at mid-sized companies. I managed to close a couple of initial deals with clients after about four months. The dollar volume of my sales was not huge, but my sales and the others from our five-person sales force kept our investors hopeful.

By osmosis, I was becoming a student of the venture capital financing game. It was 2004 and there was still some good activity with angel and other investors "out there." I was assigned to be the back up contact person to our CFO who traveled extensively and was known for avoiding voice mails and text messages. He was the principal contact with a venture capital firm we were courting. That VC firm had some history with projects in the medical space so our CEO thought the VC firm's liaison would like me.

This back-up job didn't deter much from my sales work and I found it infinitely more interesting. My role was basically secretarial to the CFO who didn't like the CEO's secretary. I would send and receive financial-related correspondence between our CFO and the VC firm. Due to my people skills, everyone started relying more and more on me to be the liaison with the VC firm. It seemed like our CFO was looking for another job or not really engaged for some reason.

As our travel service firm struggled, and the CFO did resign, I was in the catbird's seat because my employer was in the process of securing another round of financing. There was no way the VC firm would fund us with our struggling sales, questionable service lines and shaky C-Level staffing. So I invited my contact at the VC firm to lunch.

I told Daniel I wanted to join his venture capital company. The idea of finding emerging companies and lending them money to expand in exchange for a piece of the action sounded like more fun than ever. He went on to explain to me the credentials of the people he worked with. They *all* had MBAs, PhDs, and years of Mergers and Acquisitions or investment banking experience. My BS degree and a few years of selling wouldn't get me in their door. They had administrative assistants who looked better on paper (and in person) than I did. I pointed out to him that his biggest business problem though was a shortage of *solid* potential deals for them to invest in. He agreed but still couldn't hire me.

That conversation set me thinking about the need for "bird-dogs" in the VC field. I did hours of library, Internet, face-to-face visits, and telephone research. I determined there may be a market for my own "bird dog" agency that introduced emerging companies, "certified," high-net-worth individuals, and investment bankers to each other. It would be slow and novel *but it might just work*, I reasoned.

I was in a position to try this because failing wouldn't be the end of the world. I could always go get a job selling somewhere. I had little overhead or debt, my current wardrobe was appropriate, and I could office out of my apartment's second bedroom. My fast Internet connection and Blackberry covered me connection-wise and my techie friend offered to build me a screaming fast, super powerful computer for ¼ of what it would cost new.

I knew it would be a slow ramp-up, so I cut back on my living costs. However, I kept my sports car because it was a big part of the image I needed to portray in the field. I wanted to be perceived just like my convertible: fast, expensive, and on the edge of dangerous.

My parents gave me a loan to help out with my first year operating and living expenses. They thought I should take another sales job, but also remembered my great success at selling Girl Scout cookies way back when. They also knew I could always get another job selling something later if this didn't work. Dad even said "Well, if this works, nobody is going to cut or change your territory ever again!"

ॐ

At first, few took me seriously. I was young and had virtually no track record as a dealmaker or broker. I worked harder than ever to introduce myself to as many emerging companies as possible. My friends wondered why I rarely came out for the evening nights on the town that we were famous for while I was in my early twenties. Instead I stayed home and worked, mostly canvassing Facebook, MySpace, LinkedIn, Twitter, Digg, and twenty other social and business networking tools. I have thousands of friends and connections on those sites and they hear from me often via my weekly, public updates.

I created my own simple web site but that was mostly just an online brochure. My new business was all about relationships and networking, not an impersonal ecommerce function. My entrepreneurs have to trust me before they'll let me "shop" their firms to the right financing group. And that takes time.

I eventually earned the trust of some emerging technical and healthcare niche start ups which had potential. Some of them had been approached by VC firms but some were just getting ready to throw their hat into those circles. In a couple of cases, I even wrested a solid lead or two from the grasp of VC firms who were moving in for the kill on various entrepreneurs. Since no money had yet exchanged hands, they were still open to suitors.

The venture capital firms were skeptical of me, but also realized I was aggressive and persuasive enough to show them some firms they may not otherwise be able to work with. I was basically running a dating service for entrepreneurs and high net worth angel investor groups. The capital firms were becoming used to the idea of paying me a research fee on the front end or a bigger finder's fee when they closed a deal to finance a new venture. Since I didn't really need any money for a year, I had patience. I don't know why I did because I was still in my twenties and had a sense of urgency like nobody I know. I guess I just could see the big picture and that motivated me to chill.

One small technology firm I had become close to was eventually funded by a VC firm that I had introduced them to. With a recession looming in early 2008, the start-up tech firm was eager to get some money on their books. They had an attractive, recession-busting technology so my VC client was pleased to get that deal done. The tech firm got funding of over $7,000,000 so my 1% fee was sweet like candy. That represented just 60% of the best year I had while a sales employee but it made me feel like I was off to a great start. I started repaying my loan to my parents and kept upgrading my wardrobe and my business entertainment budget.

Today I still have a combined daily total of at least fifty new phone calls, emails, social networking invitations or in-person connections with people I don't know and, better yet, with people I *do* know or am familiar with. I sense that my second full year in this game will net me two or three similar deals to my first one! I love the action!

Even in periods of investor caution, I can dig out and find emerging companies and ready investors. In tough times when the investors are cautious and want to hold on to their money, they *can* be "sold" by appealing to their fear of losing that "one hot deal" that their competitor will hear about on my next call. Bad economies are often rife with bargains and flush firms that still need to make good, strategic deals.

I am building a great reputation in the space of emerging software and healthcare device communities. I am getting known as "the woman who knows everyone." The entrepreneurs trust me fairly quickly because I am not the actual venture capital company, because I can talk their talk, and mostly because I am just loveable old (young) me! The VCs are open to hearing from me because they think I may know something of value that they don't.

I love this life because I now feel like I am in control of my own territory, time, and earnings. This is not the life for many because I kept my initial cost of living low, got a favorable loan from relatives and have a very high extrovert and woo rating. I wouldn't recommend anyone without those assets to jump in like I did. But the time was right and luck, as they say, is the intersection of hard work and preparedness. I am making my own luck and look forward to doing two or three deals next year!

෨෫

For Vicki's favorite web sites
please see www.growmedia.com.

# 26

# Determine What You Want and Need

## CIO Leonard Levels Out

Paul,

My career represented the American dream. For six years, I was a Vice President of Information Technology, reaching that level after "only" 24 years of industry experience. Then it all went down the toilet in about 24 hours. Here is my story:

≈❧

After drifting around in low-wage jobs following my Army stint, I applied for a computer operator job at a large insurance company. Having exposure to some primitive computers in the Army apparently made me moderately hirable. It certainly wasn't my haircut they liked!

My graveyard shift in the computer operations area lasted about a year until I was promoted to the evening or "swing" shift. They call it "graveyard" for a good reason! I nabbed a daytime slot one year after that.

The work I did became boring pretty quickly but I watched and learned from the other people in the fast-growing data processing department. I determined I could earn more money by becoming a programmer so I enrolled in night school at the community college in the data processing and computer programming major. The school's equipment was akin to what I had seen in the Army.

Eventually I got my Associate Degree and applied for a Programmer Trainee position. My good internal work history in the company, my ability to relate to lots of different kinds of folks, and the company's need for warm bodies to do programming helped me land a coding job.

Over the years I rose up through Programmer Trainee to Programmer Analyst to Sr. Programmer Analyst to Systems Analyst I, II, and III and finally to a Project Leader title. The company continued to throw money at the department which got the new name, "Information Technology." That helped me keep earning promotions in the 1980s and 1990s.

None of my promotions came by accident. I planned my entire career growth from what I had learned in the Army. I targeted the people who could hire me for the next level hire and got to know them. I gravitated to projects which showcased my skills and desires. I actually paid attention to structure, chain of command, and internal politics back in the military. I used that knowledge of how big organizations work to my advantage.

❧

Internal power struggles for departmental control started slowing my promotions. As more and more millions of dollars were being thrown at "IT Solutions," the more bureaucratic things became. I was on fire with ambition but kept hitting my head on the ceiling.

When that headhunter called about joining an IT department at a fast-growth bank in our city, I listened. I had earned a BS degree in night classes and I had a good start on my weekend MBA program. I took the interview and was impressed by the bank's fast growth culture and true commitment to IT innovation.

My new function there was to head the firm's Project Management Office. It reported directly to the Assistant Vice President of Information Technology. I loved that job because many of the bank's big automation projects flowed through me. It was a hot seat which offered exposure to many powerful Business Unit Heads throughout the enterprise. My long hours at work and my MBA studies made me a stranger at home, but I felt I was going places. I was thrilled to finally earn my MBA.

ॐ

Three years later, Bob retired from the AVP slot and I got his job. Four years after that I was promoted to the VP of IT position. I was the poster boy for pulling yourself up by the bootstraps.

The VP of IT job was fun. I liked the status and influence I had over my department of 275 employees. My skilled team of guys and gals made many changes and built a strong ecommerce and Internet presence for the bank. Plus we got the right amount of old, legacy applications killed.

I fought all the battles typical of an organization that size. Too many people thought IT was the enemy. "An expensive hobby," was how the Chairman of the Board of the family owned bank described what we did. He was older and didn't understand what it took to keep his inherited bank competitive. Other than that, things were going well until my old friend Pete called.

Pete was once my boss at the insurance company. We'd kept in touch as golfing buddies but I had passed him up job status-wise. The last that I had heard he was still just a middle manager at the insurance company.

Over some drinks and cigars at the country club Pete enticed me to consider joining the dot-com start-up company he had signed on with. His firm looked like it was on track to create several millionaires by 2004 or so. My compensation at the time was over six figures, so I was cautious.

But Pete knew me well enough to know I needed another world to conquer. He sensed correctly how my move to the bank put me into a situation of limited advancement due to the fact my last name didn't match the family that owned the place.

After just 24 hours of research and a couple of quickie interviews, I had earned an offer from the 31-person start-up company. Their business plan was strategic, their financing secure, their management team appeared solid. They agreed to match my present income plus adding an extra $400,000 worth (upon maturation) of stock options. That caught my eye because the bank had nothing like that. Terms of my offer were that I had to give them an answer quickly. I agreed.

The short version of what happened next is that we secured a third round of financing and grew to over one-hundred employees. We started getting some market share and were building good brand recognition. The firm had survived the Y2K Hangover, Dot-Bomb Crash, the post-9/11 environment, Y2K, Enron, WorldCom and other business-killers. But technology was changing in their niche and by 2004 the firm's servers and furniture got grabbed by the sheriff's department for back taxes. My last paycheck bounced.

ह◆

The bank had filled my old job and didn't want to bring me back as consultant due to the "negative message that might send to the staff." I switched my accounts to a new bank. At 49 years old I couldn't afford to retire nor did I want to if I even had that option. My family and my creditors had come to rely on my healthy salary which had been fueled by a healthy ego. I needed to stir up some income fast or there would be trouble by Christmas.

I contacted all of my friends and contacts in the industry and they were all supportive but none of them knew of a job for me. The kids were too entrenched in school to even think about relocation so I started to panic.

In three weeks, I landed an interview with a small software company that had a staff of forty people. They had a nice ten-year history, a solid base of customers, and steady profitability. They made an offer which I turned down, much to the surprise of my wife Lisa. The money was less than I was used to, but I didn't like the job's "vibe".

I could tell from the interviews and meetings with their owner how they wanted me for the "brand" I represented. They wanted to trot me out on their sales calls in order to sell more software in their insurance company niche. My former employer the insurance company was a customer of theirs. But I wanted to be a manger, not some pre-sales image guy, so I declined the offer.

Lisa began surfing jobs from her office and noticed an

IT manager position at www.usa.gov. She used her office computer because she knew some of what she was finding wouldn't fit my ego.

She told me about an opening at a federal government agency in a city 30 minutes from our home. I explained to her how I was overqualified for that position and why and how I was not a fit for a "government job" even though they were hiring. I told her how it paid much less than what I was used to and how it wouldn't utilize my real abilities. She quietly listened to my rant and after I was done, pointed out how we were going be using the kids' college savings funds for grocery money in less than three months.

After a two-month interview cycle, I received and eagerly accepted the job offer from this federal agency. I manage a 64-person IT department and work weekdays from 8 to 5 with an hour for lunch. In the old days, some of my CIO peers might laugh at me for the "status downgrade" I took. But, several of those folks are unemployed so I don't hear much.

After many months on the job, I was able to implement many plans and cost-saving improvements. There are numerous budget and political realities in my new shop but we are making some good progress due to the high quality of people who work there. I would match this group of people with *any* that I worked with in the private sector.

My responsibility is less, my pay is less, the pace is slower, our equipment is cheaper, the environs less fancy and the budget is as tight as a drum. But, guess what? I love it! My glamorous and wild career rides were fun, but this is good, steady work for this point in my life.

At home we cut many fluff items out of the budget. For instance, we dumped our family membership to the expensive health club and canned the tennis lessons for the girls.

We now take them to the public park tennis courts on weekends and teach them ourselves. They enjoy spending the time with Lisa and me verses getting dropped off to do time with some has-been tennis pro. Now I actually use the treadmill at home instead of worrying if I'll ever get to the health club. I have lost 20 pounds, my blood pressure is normal and my family is closer than ever.

෨

I'll be the first to tell you my ego was well-fueled by all the promotions and growth I enjoyed over the past two decades. And I was proud of where I'd come from and where I had arrived. I was so proud that I began to feel entitled. I felt I deserved everything I had earned at the top level—the pay, the perks, etc. I did deserve it because I earned that status with little help from others. BUT, I had started to feel like I was superior to others who hadn't reached my level. Getting knocked around in the job market taught me about humility and it was a very educational time. Watching the Creditor Buzzards circling overhead does something to a guy.

But now the inflated ego is in check and has been replaced by a deep sense of gratitude. I am thrilled to serve in the job which indirectly helps thousands of people whether they know it or not. My employer appears to be thrilled with me which is a nice feeling I hadn't felt in a long time. Job transitions can be very educational if you listen to what those events tell you.

෨

For Websites which helped Leonard out,
please go to www.growmedia.com.

# 27

# Change Your Game Plan

## Ex-Coach Sells Youth Fitness

*The Business Beat* —October 17
**Ex-Jock Joe Johnson Executes a New Game Plan**

Joe Johnson was the starting quarterback on his high school *and* college teams. He played for an NAIA level college in Florida where his team placed second in the nation in 1991. After college Joe came back home to Texas and went on to work in assistant and then head coaching jobs at his old high school. His teams secured five all-city championships, one runner-up state football championship and one state football championship. Johnson's winning attitude has helped him win in his teaching and coaching and at his foray into entrepreneurial ventures.

"I make my customers into winners," brags Johnson. After a very successful 14-year teaching and coaching career, he shocked his coworkers three years ago by announcing his resignation. Nobody in the teachers' lounge understood

Johnson's decision since he was at the top of his game at one of the state's top twenty high schools.

After a slow start, Johnson's Youth Fitness Center has taken off. He recently added more square footage to his gym in a light industrial zone in the city's Southwest Industrial Park.

"Fitness is more important than ever for this generation of kids. They are growing up with video games and computer learning and being very sedentary. We get those kids moving." Apparently their Baby Boomer and Gen X parents agree.

"Two career households have strong incomes but weak availability to spend time doing sports with their kids. Time-strapped parents of kids aged 5 to 18 are our main customers." Johnson explains.

"Our customers may or may not already be in soccer, baseball, football or dance, but parents still enroll their kids with me to be sure their kids are getting balance." His young customers get fit through a wide variety of structured and unstructured activities and games at his center. Johnson says his rule is that his clients have to be moving most of the time while they are at the center. With the dozens of activities and programs his center offers, this does not appear to be a hard thing to do.

Trampolines, gymnastic equipment, parachutes, obstacle courses, rock walls, rope courses, punching bags, kid-sized "gerbil cages," balls of all shapes and sizes, an indoor batting cage, a soccer goal, a golf net, spinning classes for kids, basketball hoops, an aerobic floor area, and even a putting green offer almost too many options.

"Parents have a hard time deciding which activity centers to get Junior involved with first," Johnson said of the many specialties offered. "But we have a progressive, skills-based program we put them through with our trainers. It is well supervised and neither the kids nor the parents need to think much."

The former coach continued, saying, "We're basically an intense Physical Education Function that supplements the public school offerings. Academics are pushing out some PE offerings at the schools these days. Learning is important; however healthy bodies support healthy minds. We don't want PE cut-backs to negatively affect children," he went on to say,

"Baby boomers grew up in schools known for strong PE and sports programs. Remember the President's Council on Physical Fitness? I think all of us remember that program which some kids hated. My gym focuses on helping kids to achieve their Presidential Physical Fitness Award. Those programs still exist and we make a big deal about those awards and their various levels. The parents get excited about it too. Everyone seems to respond well to our Wall of Fame where we post all achievements by the kids related to the President's Council. We call it the President's Wall and it is covered with photos and statistics. The schools just don't have the time, budgets or resources to do what we do. Concerned parents know this and are willing to pay us for what we do well."

For his staff, Johnson hires college students who are PE and Athletic Trainer majors. He can't pay these students much for their part-time work so he compensates them by improving their leadership and coaching skills, building their resumes and references, plus helping them network into real jobs through Johnson's connections in the region. Several of his former employees have obtained assistant coaching jobs across the state, he says.

Johnson acknowledges how building his gym's membership and cash flow took much longer than he'd planned.

"I was naïve about how much my community visibility would help with recruiting new customer members. Thousands of people knew of me from our teams' football successes, and I thought that would translate to hundreds of fitness customers. That was wrong. And that error combined with tough economic times nearly sunk this venture early on. I took a second mortgage on the house, borrowed from friends, family and one angel investor. Even 'Uncle MasterCard' patched me through a couple of Tight Payroll Fridays. I don't recommend *that*! Profit and Loss statements are nerve-wracking for a guy who was used to a steady paycheck."

His gym also helped make ends meet in the early days by renting space to fencing, karate, and square dance clubs after its 9:00 PM closing time for the youth.

"Those partners who need a cheap facility really help me with cash flow. We still host several groups that way and I owe a lot to their loyalty. We are now offering fitness activities aimed at helping niche sports communities in adult fitness too. An example is a light fitness class for square dancers. The clientele is more senior adults and they are just as interested in fitness as anyone. But they aren't the types who would ever do the big health club scene. We love hosting activity groups of any flavor."

### Business Development

The former football star mentioned how he actively knocks on the doors of corporate wellness directors at companies in order to build awareness of his services. He offers discounts to corporate employees who come to him through their employers' benefit programs. He also works with corporate training directors encouraging them to use his facility for company team-building business-related events which involve physical activity. The coach's indoor rope course is popular for this.

Johnson's deep roots in the community certainly helped grow his business. He personally contacted hundreds of people with sports club or school athletic affiliations. He has formed dozens of specialty groups on what he calls "The Big Four Social Networking Sites." His facility is prevalent on those web sites where people gather.

"One of my part-time employees, Laura, is a college athlete who is a fitness-oriented sales and marketing major. She is really outgoing and has built up online social network groups of thousands of local people interested in sports, sports socializing, youth fitness, coaching, athletic training and the like. She got a friend of hers to record video of many of our programs in action. They edited the piece beautifully and it is available to be seen on YouTube.com where it gets a good number of hits. I am told YouTube is 'the second largest search engine out there' so we are pleased with its traffic and think it helps. I gave her and her friend $200 each as a bonus. Now I have a nearly professional online commercial. It gets hundreds of hits per week and it costs me basically nothing."

He says Laura is a master at driving traffic to those videos and interest groups on LinkedIn and through her intense blogging on Wordpress.com. The coach says he's considering a Skype.com-based, weekly fitness call in show with an emphasis on local athletics. He stated how this is a tool which allows video conferencing over the net for free for anyone who has simply downloaded that tool.

"It is ironic how having Laura sit at the computer for hours on end results in dozens of young customers getting *away* from their computers and onto their feet," the coach said with a wink.

His facility competes for members with the splashy, big budget multi-million-dollar facilities. He explained how those huge centers are "friendly competition" and offer everything to everyone, but they have 'revolving door' staffs. He explained how those facilities are run like the major corporate businesses they are.

"I have waiting lists of student athletes who want to be employees for me, including kids from those big clubs. These potential employees are the kids of parents I have known for years. They want to work here under our philosophy. We'll never offer a huge pool or aquatic programs like the Y or the private country clubs, but I'll compare my staff and my reputation for building young athletes with anyone, any day!" The coach hasn't lost his competitive spirit.

Despite the slow start to his venture, Johnson is clearly enjoying life. He likes being his own boss while helping young people live up to their full potential.

"I wasn't laid off from the school system – I had just topped out. The school board was very sad to see me go and tried to get me to stay. However, I sensed my great ride there had peaked and I had a unique brand name in this city. I decided to take a risk and see if I could solicit funds and customers for my *own* venture instead of fundraising for the schools."

It appears Johnson has thrown another game-winning touchdown because he is thrilled with his company's classes which are full of kids who are on their way to better health. He is now exploring a location for a potential second facility in the city's north side.

"Its all about building a team, fundamentals and execution," said Coach and CEO Johnson before jogging off to bark some suggestions to some of his youthful charges who were doing a basketball drill. His booming voice was a reminder of the imprint Coach Johnson is having on the fitness of hundreds of young people in our city.

ॐ

For Web Sites Joe used to set up his business, please visit **www.growmedia.com**.

# 28

# Find Your Hidden Job Market

## Banker Patti Halts Her Job Hopping

Thanks for asking me to speak to your MBA class tonight and thank-you Professor Olson for making a recording of this so we can transcribe it later.

❧

As you know from my introduction, I'm Patti and I don't have an advanced degree so I'm not very comfortable speaking to you tonight. But, perhaps we can all learn from each other as we discuss careers and job hunting. Professor Olson is one of our long-term customers and he thought my personal story may be helpful to you as your graduation approaches.

A couple of years ago, I was fed up with the banking world. In a four-year period, I quit one bank, got laid off from another, and then went through two mergers. This was shocking since my parents both worked uninterrupted in the banking industry for a combined total of nearly seventy years.

After college, my folks encouraged me to interview with large banks, feeling they would be stable employers for me. I accepted a job with a large downtown bank and loved my role as a personal banker trainee. My personality and skills enabled me to progress quickly and I was soon allowed to make bigger loans and was moved to one of the suburban branches. My salary was not huge but I felt like I was on a "fast track."

My second annual review came and I got a modest increase complete with lots of encouragement about my future. They promised to move me into small business lending or mortgage banking, telling me those areas had higher income potential. With that encouragement, I got a more expensive apartment and bought a new, low-end Audi. My parents thought I was insane to incur so much debt. Ah, the Irrefutable Wisdom of Youth!

Then along came the merger. Well, it was more like a take-over but everyone kept calling it a "combining of interests." The national banking company we merged with treated us like idiots. They were in a hurry to acquire smaller banks during the down economy. I correctly sensed that all bets were off for my future. Nobody would remember the promises which had been made to me regarding my career path.

They still needed good staff to run the place, but I couldn't believe all the new policies and procedures and forms and added layers of decision-makers and committees. Decisions of any consequence were usually run past some off-site managers. My peers seemed unmotivated and layoffs were rumored.

Over a year of this passed, and I was unable to acquire

any new responsibilities. My late salary review was laughable. My new boss stated how one-to-two percent increases were now standard because of the serious recession which was "on the horizon." Tough times made the employer re-evaluate all costs and personnel. He mumbled something about my being lucky to avoid a layoff.

Well I didn't much care for the new sheriff in town so I quit and joined another local bank as a Small Business Lender Trainee. My folks looked at me like I was from Mars when I told them about my *Next* New Job.

I had over three years of experience and was still a trainee! But I was just glad to be out of the old situation. What I quickly realized however, was my new situation was similar to my old one. And this new employer was filled to the brim with corporate politics.

At home over Thanksgiving dinner I brought up the question of corporate politics. My parents admitted how they did have plenty of corporate politics in their day but they "suffered through it." They encouraged me to hang in there and survive by making nobody mad at me and told me to avoid back-stabbers who were hunting for peers to stomp on. Wise advice but at the time I felt their attitude of *put up and shut up* seemed like they were playing the part of middle school guidance counselor. That is what *their* generation had to do—didn't they know I was a proud Gen Y / Millennial? We live to text and text to live, change jobs at a moment's notice, and feel that *there is always a tomorrow!*

ॐ

As unbelievable as it sounds, my new bank also became part of a merger. This time, *we* did the acquiring of a local bank system which was of a similar size to ours. Everyone expected some staff shuffling due to the obvious duplication of services. My lending activity was flat in the next few months due to the "wait and see" merger confusion amongst our clients.

The new entity eventually decided to close our facility as it was too close to a nicer branch office of the company we had acquired. I assumed I would be moving to our downtown office. Well, you know what they say about the word "assumed."

The new entity's strategic planners group decided there were too many people in my job classification. Laying me off was "justified" because I was too new there to have built up a clientele. Those were the facts, but the kicker was all the "good-old-boys" got to stay on. I was bitter but moved on and I was getting too good at these separations.

There I was with a very choppy employment history, overextended on my apartment and my car, 26 years-old, single, and without a job. I could hear my folks moaning about my perilous career track all the way from my hometown which was 80 miles away.

Fortunately, the bank gave me a "special situation" severance package of three months' worth of pay. Since I had joined them under a different pretense just seven months previous, I must have fit some check-off box on their matrix of "humane" merger procedures. I signed a document which stated I could not sue them regarding this layoff nor could I tell anyone about my "hush money." I took it and ran.

Next, I wanted to avoid all bank employment if humanly possible. However, my entire, post-college work experience had been in banking. I applied for many jobs outside of banking but got little response. I couldn't believe I was pigeon-holed at such a young age.

After two months of little job-hunting progress, I visited a job coach to try to breathe some life into my search. She helped me realize there are many major corporate employers, including educational and government entities in our Kansas City area which have internal or captive credit unions. I had never considered the idea of working for a credit union since all past bank employers held snobby attitudes toward them.

After learning more, I got a bit excited. I suddenly had over a dozen new potential employers in town! But I then learned most credit unions are very stable and have little, if any staff turnover. None of them appeared to have any open positions that were anywhere close to fitting me. With my severance pay nearly gone, my coach suggested a *Blitzkrieg Job Hunt.*

It was time to get in front of the people who could make things happen. I networked heavily on FaceBook but also went to the FedEx Office Store/Kinkos to create a business-card-sized "Mini Resume." I am handing out one to each of you:

**Patti Jones: Financial Services Professional**
*Seek to utilize 4 years' of successful lending experience in Personal, Commercial, and Mortgage areas;*
*Well-Connected; Personable; Team Player*
*"Rainmaker" who bring in new loans*
*Affordable compensation*
*Available now as a: Temp, Perm/Direct Hire, Contractor*
*Patti_Jones@growmedia.com mobile: 555.555.5555*

I visited the lobbies at all the credit unions in the area and I'd say, in a bit of an 'entitled' tone,

"I need to speak to your Branch Manager." Sometimes they'd ask "What is this regarding?" And I'd reply slightly annoyed with something like,

"It's a business matter that needs her attention."

I got screened out only twice. Most of the time they didn't ask what I wanted, thinking I was just a pissed-off member-customer.

My job coach told me this approach would *definitely* kill my chances at some firms. But, she said I might also end up talking to a lot more hiring managers than by searching in traditional ways. Each of the seven times I got through to the manager, I'd always use the same elevator speech my job coach and I created. It went like this:

> "Ms. Branch Manager, if this office needs to grow its lending portfolio, I know of an enthusiastic, person who can open new business, even in this economy."
> Then I'd pause and finally say, "That person is me."

Then I would hand them my little business card resume and say *nothing*. After reading my card twice, they would *always* give me one of these responses:

1. *We are not hiring right now.* But, I got a call back from one firm where the branch manager said that while looking me right in the eyes. It turned out that *her* branch wasn't hiring but another one was. She just didn't know about that but had handed my card to Human Resources.

2. *You have to apply online – through Human Resources.* When I got this line I would say something like "HR is not the hiring manager are they? Wouldn't you as

a Branch Manager prefer a short, casual conversation right now with an upbeat lending officer like me who is *not* just an order taker? Isn't that the kind of person you want to generate lending activity for you?

Then I'd shut up again and wait for their reply. Seven elevator speeches and follow-ups like this got me three sit-down chats with managers. Those chats ranged from 5 to 55 minutes in length. None of those three Credit Unions had jobs posted.

3. *Let's sit down and chat a bit* Victory! These are the three victories I just mentioned. I didn't have to sell my way into these other than my original pitch.

My assertive style and little business card resume were what my job coach called the "differentiator." I did end up getting a position with a credit union which did *not* have a job vacancy posted. I got a lot of funny looks and rejection along the way but nobody ever punched me.

Role-playing with my job coach gave me the guts to sell myself this way. Previously I don't think I was the kind of person who could do that. But, I adapted because I feared my new car could be repossessed. If I lost my car that way I'd never get a job at a financial organization. I had tried to sell it but was upside down on its worth. So, I opted for the guerilla job hunt strategies instead.

My credit union employer used to be captive to the largest insurance company in town but now it is broadening its services and is adding branch locations throughout the city. Its assets are much smaller than any financial institution I previously worked for, yet their stability seems better. It feels like I am working in my old, small, hometown and I love it.

&

To summarize, you'll soon be hitting the job market soon with your advanced degrees. I encourage you to *Look Beyond the Obvious* in your job hunt. The recession is still slowing the job market in KC. But, if you look behind the curtain you can find something you may not have even considered before.

*Everyone Else* is surfing the obvious job posts on the internet. What can *you* do that is unique which helps you stand out? What is **NOT** being done by your dozens or hundreds of job seeking competitors? What results have *you* achieved that nobody else can bring?

Best wishes out there. If any of you are going straight to entrepreneurship after you get your degree, please see me—I have some great lending packages for small business!

ॐ

For websites which Patti used in
her job search, see **www.growmedia.com**.

# 29

# Be Open to New Opportunities

## Nurse Assistant Offers Care-for-Hire

Paul,

    With your background in sales, resumes and job coaching, I hope you can give me some constructive criticism on the following letter. It is the draft of what I may use to "market" my services. I'm not sure I need a letter at all because I am almost too busy without any advertising. But, my husband thinks I need some hype like this. What do you think?

    I feel called to this kind of work. I never would have imagined I could earn a living doing something I love this much!

    This "business" is not about money for me, although it is nice to have. With my premature retirement, my husband's income alone won't cover our bills. And he is set to retire in 2011. I am now earning more than I did on a full-time basis at the luxury nursing home I was separated from. And I only "work" part-time!

This work lets me do what I do best: Helping people. Now I don't have to spend my time lifting them or being on my feet for eight hours at a time. Plus, I love the flexibility I now have.

Let me know how you think I can improve the following letter. Is it too long? Thanks so much for your encouragement and support!

Peace!

Alice

&

*Dear Clergy Person or Hospital Chaplain,*

This letter is to introduce you to my services which I believe compliment yours. When families are involved in a medical crisis, you offer comfort to them and their loved ones. I also do that in my role as a Care Companion.

For twenty-seven years, I worked in numerous Tennessee hospitals, clinics, and nursing homes as a (Certified) Nurse Assistant. I have worked beside doctors, nurses, and all other health-care professionals, with all types of patients in all types of settings, including hospice.

My work involved the hands-on patient care and support that other health care professionals did not or would not do. Everyone told me I have the best bedside manner around. Patients often ended up communicating through me to their doctors.

Two years ago I resigned when my feet and back could no longer handle the physical demands required by my job. That's when I fell into my work as a Care Companion.

When my long-time friend Margaret was admitted to the Intensive Care Unit, I stayed by her bed night and day until her West Coast family could finally arrive. Margaret's husband died long ago so she would have otherwise been all alone. When they arrived, her family thanked me profusely for the time I had spent with Margaret. I was glad I was there for her because she passed on just two weeks later.

When I was keeping vigil over Margaret, I got to know some of the other families who were also supporting loved ones in the Intensive Care Unit. During a visitor lounge chat, one family asked me to stay at their mother's bed side while they had to leave to attend to the needs of one of their children.

While I spent time with their mother it occurred to me how my ability to just "be there" was a gift I could offer to people. I didn't have a job and my kids were long gone from my home. And my husband had a full-time job so I was readily available and looking for something to do.

I stayed with that family's mother for four hours and was happy to help. Upon their return, the family insisted on paying me for my time. I was embarrassed that they even offered to pay me and promptly declined. That family must have been tickled because I heard later how they had told several people in the ICU lounge about me. I didn't care for that kind of attention.

ॐ

One thing led to another and I got a reputation for being a person who could "be present" at the ICU or other hospital floors. It is so hard for people with jobs or busy families to stop everything and be present to support their ill loved ones. People ended up telling their clergy persons about me!

Now, when I am invited, I spend about thirty hours a week visiting geriatric care facilities, intensive care units, the children's hospital, and clients in their own homes. My role is very simple. I am there to support the patient when their family can't. With families scattered to the winds these days, people really seem to need my services.

I never provide any form of spiritual advice, tax or legal advice, counseling, or medical functions. My role is STRICTLY non-medical support. In a hospital that means just being there and being an advocate for the patient. I know how to ask nurses for their help and they love having me around.

I will pray with my clients *if they ask me to*, or hum hymns *if they request it*. Mostly we just talk if they can or I hold their hands and read to them. I especially like sharing *Chicken Soup for the Soul* stories with my clients.

When I am a Care Companion in a person's home, I do anything they want me to do that is non-medical. I can shop for them or take them shopping. I can cook, clean, talk, play games, drive them to the pharmacy or to the church or wherever. One family said it was OK for me to take their grumpy 84 year-old father to the keno parlor once a week! I didn't like that too much but my client was thrilled.

My clients who are still living in their homes seem to be able to stay there longer and avoid nursing homes due to my services. Their families love this.

There are big and medium-sized companies who offer the same kind of in-home or in-hospital services which I provide. I know many of these people and they do a great job. People tell me they like to hire me instead because they know exactly who they will get each time to deliver the services—me!

❧

So hopefully my story will inform you more about my services. I write to you simply to inform you of my availability should any of your parishioners ever need this service. I have all the proper bonding and insurance required to do this kind of service and feel blessed I can be there for my clients.

My contact information is listed below as are several references and testimonials. My services are offered on a flexible basis regarding costs. If I can do some short term coverage for people who may not be able to pay, I will.

I have spent my whole career preparing for this kind of work. Please let me know if you think I can help someone who needs it.

Thank you for your time and *your* work!

Alice Black

*Alice,*

*It is a nice, heartfelt letter. We'll need to shorten it up quite a bit and determine how you can best deliver it to your clergy-person community. Your strategy to approach them is a solid one.*

*Let's check into the idea of forming a group on LinkedIn that tracks with what you are trying to accomplish.*

*Paul*

࿊

Internet resources which were helpful to Alice
can be found at **www.growmedia.com**.

# 30

# Move Beyond Rejection

## Major Mike Makes His Own Job

Paul,

After 21 years of honorable service in the United States Air Force, I thought the private sector would readily scoop me up as an employee. But, after months of post-retirement job hunting, I was still unemployed. It seemed like the business world didn't know how to relate to me. So, instead of hunting for a job, I became an employer! Here is my story:

❧

My retirement came after a decorated career with USAF. At my peak in the service, I had a structure of nearly 100 direct and indirect reports. I led numerous task forces, supervised a cadre of network technology professionals at two separate bases, earned my MBA, and was recognized for my work at a European staging base during Operation Iraqi Freedom. I had a stellar service record, proven management abilities, technical savvy, and strong linguist skills.

*Still*, I couldn't capture the attention of the hiring officials in the corporate sector. True, my experience was specific to military settings, but I *thought* companies need good managers—good raw material like me. I managed some very complex functions and *lives depended* upon my crew's effectiveness. You can't say that about an internal auditor!

During my few corporate interviews, the employers implied most of their mangers were promoted from within. Since I didn't have that internal company knowledge of my competitors, I never got past the front door. This was a very frustrating time in my life since I used to have significant responsibility in the military.

Fortunately, my military pension and my wife Myesha's good job allowed me a more leisurely job search than some people could afford.

ॐ

I researched, studied, and researched some more. I got very good at spotting employment trends online. An area meatpacking plant always seemed to have openings for production workers. Noting that trend, I invited an ex-USAF friend to lunch. After his separation, Joel landed a job as a Software Developer with that large firm.

I drilled him for his thoughts on his employer's constant *Help Wanted* advertising. He summed it all up in one word: "Turnover." He said extremely high turnover amongst the laborers consistently slowed production and threatened production quotas. Shortages of labor only made the management of the plant run production lines faster, which in turn increased turnover. It was a *Catch 22*, he explained.

Many of the production workers were of Latino background. Some key managers spoke some Spanish but were not fluent. Joel said there was a climate of distrust, disconnection and dismay throughout the facility. Needs of the production employees were too often ignored in part or all together. Constant rehiring and retraining kept the plant from operating smoothly.

As Joel described the situation, I was reminded of a project I handled while in the Air Force where I had to build trust and capability quickly for the new arrivals at our deployed unit. I fixed the problem through my command group and beyond and was recognized and praised for my group's increased morale and productivity. The key had been to simply recognize people's paradigm upon their arrival and then be very clear about expectations. It was really just about communication.

Based on my past successes, I knew I could improve the situation at Joel's meatpacking plant. This confidence was also due to my Spanish linguist skills and my proven management aptitude.

I pumped Joel for as much "big-picture" recon as he could give, and I worked up a proposal for the plant's management. When I had a brief but strategic plan in hand, I targeted a Line Manager whose name I got from his listing on LinkedIn. com. Next, I called him through the plant's main switchboard. I left one voice mail requesting five of his minutes "to demonstrate a way to increase his production."

He didn't know me from Adam, and I had no background to make this kind of claim. But I had nothing to lose so I felt empowered. I got to "go to school" on this whole process. I left the manager a message in both Spanish and English.

It took over a week for me to actually catch him on the phone. I suspected his Caller ID displayed my phone number 20 times when I called, missed him, *and left no message.*

People are busy and get dozens of voice mails so I felt I'd stand out by *not* leaving a voice mail. He probably called me back simply wondering who the hell was so persistent and what was so damn important.

I met with him at the loading dock gate one day at the end of his shift. He looked tired and stressed. Instead of a sales pitch I briefly empathized with how tired he looked. Then he dumped on me how everyone inside was working too hard. That gave me the opening to offer him help with his staff's retention on a contingency basis. His firm would only need to pay me if my ideas worked. That got his attention.

Due to my internal reference of Joel, my professional conduct, my well-prepared handout, and my dogged persistence, he agreed to run my ideas past his boss the Floor Manager.

Two weeks passed with no news but there was an article in our local paper describing raids by the United States Immigration and Customs Enforcement in other regional cities. The local plant was mentioned as "possibly being suspect" of employing undocumented workers. That charge was later fiercely denied by the plant's corporate office in another city. Due to industry stresses like this my timing appeared to be fortunate.

❧

Some of the management team at the plant called to invite me to present some ideas. I kept my meeting with them in a Q and A format rather than a boring PowerPoint presentation. I didn't want to look like some fancy consultant. I admitted early on how I knew nothing about their industry but did briefly tell them of my staffing issue successes in the military.

I told them that if they were to bring me in, I'd simply serve as a liaison—not a representative of management. I wasn't going to be a production worker either. Both sides could therefore consider me safe and I would simply be there to build trust in the organization.

❧

After a week of deliberation by them, they brought me in for a trial week as an ombudsman primarily. The plant already had some bilingual supervisors and a good HR person, but unlike them I simply spent most of my time floating around the production areas. I took breaks with the workers and was accessible when they were coming on and off their shifts.

After a week, management agreed to keep me around for one more month, not due to any real progress, but instead due to the concise and highly strategic report I put together based on their strengths, weaknesses, opportunities and threats (SWOT). They were impressed with my recon but should have expected that from a military guy like me!

I spent about 20 hours a week on the floor. Any more than that would have been *overkill* (pun intended). I worked to get to know dozens of workers and continued to do my reconnaissance. I went to occasional management meetings to learn about issues from their side of the fence. More and more people began telling me about problems and even added their own solutions which were often spot on.

All I eventually did was help all parties to communicate and be knowledgeable of the needs of the other group. And then small fixes started being made. Fixes which I had only *facilitated*, not fixes which *I* had suggested.

After some time at this, our workers became our best

recruiters. They began to feel like management was listening and invited their friends to apply for work at our facility. We still had big problems, but the "hire-train-lose" cycle was slowing and the "don't apply here" reputation appeared to be disappearing.

ə❧

The plant management now has me on a steady retainer so I am my own consulting company. We all know the reason this works is that I am not an employee of the plant. My financial retainer is not huge, but the year-long engagement they are discussing will easily bypass my former military pay!

So now I am an employer. Instead of looking for a job, I am looking for employees because the home office of the plant wants me to duplicate my efforts at some of their other plants.

My attorney and accountant helped me create a "Limited Liability Corporation." They showed me how to get the proper types of errors and omissions and liability insurance. I used the **Service Corps of Retired Executives (SCORE)** to evaluate and help me build my business plan so I am not just shooting from the hip. That group is well-connected and is an amazing pool of talent! They offered the best free service I could ever imagine. I am now all set to add staff and expand into other locations for my client.

One year ago I would have never imagined I would have gone from a Command Center to "Carcass Central." But, here I am building my own corporate consulting practice.

Instead of getting rejected by potential employers, I now help employees to fit into the companies that need their help. I got here by simply being strategic in my approach and leveraging the resources I have. For too long I played by the rules and my job search went nowhere. Now I am having more fun than ever and thank my outside-the-box thinking for that.

᷂

For websites which were helpful to Mike, please see **www.growmedia.com**.

# SECTION 2

# Your TwitterVator Speech

# Your TwitterVator Speech

# Step 1

## *What* Are You Selling?

**B**efore you can exchange your services, skills, or knowledge for compensation, you have to know *what* you are selling. Many people assume a hiring manager, a human resources person, or a potential client will know from your resume (or some other magical way) just where you fit into their organization. **Wrong!**

The following simple exercise will help you know what skills, abilities, experience and passions you should be selling "out there." I often ask my coaching clients "Where do you fit?" This exercise can help you determine that. Answer the questions in a separate notebook using phrases or bullet points. Avoid long sentences, paragraphs or essays:

1. What are your personal and professional characteristics and attributes (ten of them or less)?

2. What are *your* (individual) three greatest work-related accomplishments?

3. What constitutes your *unique* work experience—what do *you* know better than most other people?

4. What are your passions behind your work? What motivates or inspires you and gives you a sense of meaning and or purpose? What (other than income) keeps you coming back?

5. What type of work-related activity gives you the most enjoyment?

Write today's date on your answers so you can track your thought progress over time.

These questions are intended to help you become more "Vocationally Introspective" than you have ever been before. If you want to know even more about determining your vocational strengths from a research standpoint, I recommend these works (which can be found at www.growmedia.com):

- *StrengthsFinder 2.0: A New and Upgraded Version of the Online Test from Gallup's, Now, Discover Your Strengths* by Tom Rath

- *StrengthQuest Discover and Develop Your Strengths in Academics, Career, and Beyond* by Donald O. Clifton and Edward (Chip) Anderson

- *Do What You Are — Discover the Perfect Career for You Through the Secrets of Personality Type* by Paul D. Tieger and Barbara Barron Tieger

# Step 2

## Graduate from "Differentiation U"

Are you trying to communicate your strengths via a 3-page resume? A popular rumor today in human resources circles is that resumes get between 8 to 15 seconds of review before its fate is decided upon. I call that *"Your 15 Seconds of Fame."* Combine that with the fact that HR departments are drowning in resumes even before a job vacancy is posted, and it is easy to see the dilemma: How do *you* stand out?

The Unique Selling Proposition (Point) was originated in the 1940's by Rosser Reeves. His definition: *"...any aspect of an object that differentiates it from similar objects"* (Wikipedia.org: Unique Selling Proposition /Point).

I believe Mr. Reeves and his advertising firm originated the USP with a focus on products (note his use of the word "object"). Since you may be competing for compensation with hundreds or perhaps thousands of other people, I suggest you apply the USP concept *to your career*. Differentiating yourself in today's workplace is critical, wouldn't you agree?

No matter how much *value* you have, you still have to sell yourself. Donald Trump is constantly selling himself even though his brand is strong. I suggest his brand is strong *because* he constantly sells himself!

The "Queens of All Branding" of course are Oprah Winfrey and Martha Stewart. Consider their mastery of "multimedia" and "merchandising" (TV, cable TV, radio, satellite radio, magazines, catalogues, retailing, websties, co-sponsoring, affiliate marketing, ecommerce, and more) and you have two branding mavens unheralded in their accomplishments.

Another pillar of personal branding is Michael Bloomberg, who according to Wikipedia's entry on him, spent $73 MILLION of his own money on print, TV, radio and online branding during his 2001, successful campaign for the New York City mayor's office.

Donald, Martha, Oprah and Michael have branded themselves at a level atypical of society. But, you can *learn* from the tireless and effective self-promotion conducted by these icons.

The concept of a career-oriented Unique Selling Proposition *is* similar to today's popular concept of "Personal Branding." But personal branding is so overused these days that I wince when I hear the phrase. In my opinion, the "Personal Branding" bandwagon is nearly worn out by the throngs of advice-givers who are stacked on top of it.

'Personal Branding Experts' ride into town on the internet and repackage the same basic information under the magical cloak of *personal branding.* They offer blogs, seminars, books, webinars, downloads, coaching, and sometimes overpriced wisdom. Buyer beware...for the price of this book *you'll pretty much have the gist* of what some Johnny-Come-Lately "experts" are peddling. Their packages might be slicker and their pitch more compelling than mine, but please *think* before you spend.

So, since you are Competing For Compensation with scads of people who also seek the attention of decision-makers that may only give you *15 Seconds of Fame,* how *do you* get noticed?

**Here's your answer:**

# Your TwitterVator Speech

As you know, Twitter.com is a social media phenomenon which is enjoying stratospheric growth. My mini-summary of Twitter is that it is a *Short, Instant Messenger to the Masses.* As a bicycle enthusiast, I enjoy reading Lance Armstrong's frequent "tweets" (short text messages) that he sends to me. He writes about his travels, his races, his Tour de France Comeback, his movie preferences, his training and even his new baby.

I shouldn't feel too special though because Lance includes nearly one million *other* people in his Tweets. With just one click on Twitter's "Follow" command, I and others get to track all the messages he sends. Or, I can track the tweets sent by any of the other millions of Twitterholics whom I choose to 'follow.'

Millions of the tweets people send *are* about what they had for breakfast, but millions of others are the front door to *very* fresh, web-based information which can help you to advance yourself or your business. The "Follow" feature lets you create a "cult following," if of course you present yourself as someone who is interesting.

Twitter has a field (box) where you can type your daily or

hourly or monthly updates. You are limited to just 140 characters per Tweet (message). But you can send as many Tweets as you want. While that freedom may be overly tempting for overly verbose types (like me), you need to remember to *stay interesting* and/or relevant. Most people don't care if it raining where you are.

This "mini-broadcast" or Mini Blog formula is having a dynamic impact on business and lifestyles. Almost everyone's Tweets add a link to another website or blog or video into their Twitter updates. It is among the freshest, most widely accepted social media mediums out there right now. Some say that because Google's search results are based on popularity over time, Twitter's updates are fresher and faster because they don't have to stand the test of popularity. You decide.

If social media is art, Twitter is its molding clay. Dozens of new uses and creative tools to use with Twitter are being put out there every month by third-party creators. There are too many new tools and third-party product developments, improvements and changes to track in a hard copy book. Things change with this tool every week so check out **www.growmedia.com** to follow some of its trends.

હ

**A TwitterVator Speech** *combines* the old-school USP, the "Elevator Speech" (where you are riding an elevator with a decision-maker and you have a minute or less to make your pitch to her), *and*, the 140-character, global reach of Twitter and other social media update tools.

This is important because your chance of riding an elevator alone with a top executive is remote. However, your chance of gaining access to *millions* of people who use social media (and according to LinkedIn.com, employees from *all* Fortune 500 companies are on their site), is high. Here is the theory *behind* the value of a TwitterVator Speech:

> *You get paid by <u>stating and doing</u> a compelling combination of your unique skills and the <u>most</u> strategic solution to a customer's or employer's problem.*

Here's the old bottom-line concept we all need to be reminded of:

> **Customers don't buy services and employers don't hire people unless they think those purchases or hires will save them money, make them money, save them time, or support their mission.**

### *Which of those value-added actions do you do?*

That question is intended to cut through it all and bluntly challenge you to get your head in the game of *getting* hired or *getting* some contract work.

Whether the employer's problem is slow accounts payable, or if the customer's problem is bags under her middle-aged eyes, or if the issue is a global health care epidemic, **you** need to bring a compelling solution to the table that you can implement.

And you had better be able to define and articulate that solution better than the guy or gal who was in line ahead of you. Remember, you are competing for work against the guy down the street as well as a couple of hundred million people from India and China.

# How *I* Market Myself

## Paul's TwitterVator Speech:

The following is *one* of the ways I market myself. I dissect it here hoping you will use its components to build your own awesome TwitterVator Speech. There is no *one* magic tool out there ensuring you will get and keep the work you desire. The TwitterVator Speech certainly isn't being touted as a sole panacea, but I think it will help!

Most *successful* employees and small business people constantly employ *a mix* of sales, PR, and marketing efforts and initiatives to keep them in work or to stay employed. A tool like this can be the main mast on your personal marketing sailboat.

Here is the foundation of my self-promotion effort *and* a breakdown of why it works inside of social media channels:

*America's Job Coach builds the careers &*

*businesses of professionals by posturing*

*them for vocational victory*

*www.americasjobcoach.com*

This 17-word, 135-character (including spaces) TwitterVator Speech will fit in Twitter's update box which asks "What are you doing right now?" It will also fit in the LinkedIn or FaceBook status update boxes as well as many other social media tools.

This pitch is also very handy for the back of a business card or to have memorized when I bump into a business acquaintance at a Happy Hour or a youth event. Since this TwitterVator Speech is a *part of me*, I am always ready when friends or strangers ask "So, what are you doing now?"

Now let's dissect my TwitterVator Speech as a way to help you build your own:

### "America's Job Coach..."

Sounds kind of global yet kind of simple, right? It communicates what I do—I coach people on job/career stuff. And do you like how it marks my territory? I bet you could use the name of your city or state for some kind of branding—or perhaps your industry? If you don't have a catchy "brand" or initial tag line like this for yourself, don't worry. You can also simply just describe yourself in a strategic, pithy manner.

### "...builds the careers & businesses..."

Again, this is simple, yet vague by design. To some, "builds" may mean getting a new or different job in the same field. Others may equate it to changing careers into a *new* field. "Build" is a word which captures the imagination and has a "feel-good" sound to it. Employed as well as unemployed people plus entrepreneurs all want to build on what they have going, don't they? Remember to include what problem you are solving and imply why someone should pay *you*.

### "...of professionals..."

Who is the subject that will benefit from your skills or knowledge? "Professionals" is quite vague by design. I have coached teachers, insurance agents, programmers, mechanics, and C-level professionals among others. Why would I want to exclude anyone? On the other hand, I also advocate for promoting yourself inside a tight niche. If you have a *specialized* knowledge, be sure to say so! Quantitative numbers would be good here (as in, how many professionals I have helped), but too much information and too many numbers can bore (and make you go beyond 140 characters).

### "...by posturing them...."

Posturing means different things to different people but generally it implies: *To position, to balance, to have an attitude, to have a "stance."* All of these actions are needed by job hunters and small business people as they leverage and market their skills. This involves broad universal appeal and yet addresses and nearly universal, individualized need. Does your TwitterVator Speech have universal appeal or at least broad appeal inside your niche?

### "...for vocational victory!"

I like to use a series of similar sounds because I think that creates sticking power in the mind. There is a lot of noise out there from thousands of job coaches or career mentors. But, 'Vocational Victory' is an elegant sounding event. It is something most everyone wants. Give your TwitterVator Speech a nice wrap up with a strong punch line!

241

# Now it's Your Turn!

Here are some helpful prompts to get you started on **your** strategic TwitterVator Speech:

- Make a long list of words and synonyms that relate to your answers to the earlier Strengths Questions. **Include** quantifiable numbers, results-sounding percentages, etc.

- On the same page, make lists of industries, companies, niches, groups, and *types* of people you know really well. What practices, processes, functions, groups, sectors etc. do you know *better* than anyone else?

- Next, list business or organizational trends or industry segments that are growing or experiencing change. Terry Jones found some changes occurring in the travel agency business as the internet was becoming more popular. The result? Travelocity.com and Kayak.com.

  - Right now, the sectors of government, health care, education, construction, and "green" (energy conserving) ventures are booming or at least "preparing" to boom. If the character from the 1967 movie, "The Graduate" were to whisper one *key word for success* into the ear of Dustin Hoffman's new graduate character nowadays, (over 40 years later), he might this time say *"insulation"* instead of *"plastics."* If you have no idea what I am talking about you need to find that movie and see it.

◻ Banking, automotive, insurance and the health care sectors are all experiencing radical changes as this was written. What solutions can you as a potential employee, contractor, or small business provide to these industries which are all going through Extreme Industry Makeovers?

- Circle about 25 proactive words from your above lists. Put them on note cards and move them around on a big surface in various orders. Be visual. Be imaginative. Play! If you want to have 50 note cards with key words or phrases on them, go ahead, but it will take more effort. Avoid paralysis by analysis! Be decisive. This is a Permanent Work in Progress...

- Lead off with an attention-getting, niche-oriented opener which identifies your expertise or early adaptor status.

- Don't worry about limiting yourself because it **may be wise to have multiple TwitterVator Speeches,** each with a varied theme and focused deep into a different niche which you can serve!

- Use action words, which have broad appeal. Move the cards around so they describe your mission, expertise, passion, results and attractiveness.

- Write the number of characters each word has in small numbers on the bottom of each individual card. That will make it easy to track how many characters you are accruing. You can also use Word Count under Tools on MS WORD or on your MAC if you are doing this on computer. Stay around twenty words and definitely under 140 characters (including the URL or blog site you will point your TwitterVator Speech toward).

- It is important that readers can click on a destination to learn more about you. This may be as simple as your LinkedIn profile or it could be a web site or a blog of your own, if it is strategic for you to have one (it IS important for small businesses and seems to be of growing importance for individuals).

- Wrap up your TwitterVator Speech using a catchy summary or "offer they can't refuse."

Write your 'working document' TwitterVator Speech below. Date it. This doesn't have to be your final draft. *There is no such thing*!

# Use Your TwitterVator Speech *Everywhere* (Eventually):

Regarding Twitter.com, I recommend NOT opening your twitter account and just blasting away with your new speech. Nobody cares. We are all human and crave a two-way, not a one-way street with regard to relationships.

FOLLOW many people on Twitter first. Just click the 'Follow' Button after you have searched and found interesting and strategic people (using the 'Find People' box). I suggest you follow at least a couple dozen others before springing your pitch to the world or commenting wildly. Get the feel for the tool first.

Typically, when you follow people, a percentage of those people start following you back. The bonus is when some of THEIR followers discover you as a result of this. It can all build incrementally and insidiously. Get the feel and the flow of the groups you join or follow. After getting the feel for what people in your group(s) are chatting about, you'll know how and when to throw your pitch.

Your TwitterVator Speech is for use far beyond just Twitter.com though. Use it with friends and relatives, with present, future and former coworkers, with strangers. Use it online, offline, on paper, on resumes, on business cards, on bus stops walls, in bathroom stalls. Well, maybe not the last one or two but you get the idea. What unique place might someone encounter your TwitterVator Speech?

Practice it. Learn it. Change it. Distribute it. Tweak it. Tweet it. It can be the foundation to your job search, your small business start up, and even your vocational/career mission in life. Too many people don't really know where they are headed in their work life. Nothing is as strong as your passion unleashed! When you name this thing, you empower it!

Your TVS is *not* about a canned, "Johnny One Note" speech. It reflects your mission, what you have done, and what you want to do. It is what gets that dialog started. But **YOU MUST** be ready to back up your TwitterVator Speech. Have stories, examples and research at hand so once the dialog starts, you can continue the conversation and DELIVER value! Be ready to tell a story about what you *have* accomplished, envision, plan and hope to do.

৵

*Consider letting America's Job Coach help create your optimal TwitterVator Speech. This could be an inexpensive yet invaluable investment in your future!*

# Section 3

# Building Your Personal

# Online Profile

# Building Your Personal Online Profile

## *Five Steps to Creating Your Online Relevance*

I highly recommend you have at least one online "social media/social networking" profile. In this day and age of Web 2.0 or Web 3.0, or whatever number we are on now, a quality online profile shows you have not been left behind. Ten years ago there was no FaceBook. Fifteen years ago most people were just starting to hear what was becoming known as "the Internet." Life changes fast so show the world you are relevant and staying with it!

A resume shows your job history and a couple of accomplishments. An online profile shows you are a little savvier yet. Your blog may demonstrate an even loftier presence by showing your contributions and value to your industry or niche (if it is well done). Blogging can allow you to build "a" reputation. You can come off as "current" and possibly even a thought leader or early adaptor for your niche. But be sure the reputation you are building is what you want it to be as you don't get a second chance to make a good first impression! And hard drives never forget!

Here is a summary of "Five Strategies to Creating Online Relevance." For many readers, the tools portion of this is highly remedial and old news. For others, it's all new stuff. However, there are some **"content and strategy nuggets"** herein which I believe will be *helpful to both groups*:

1. Have a strategic business-like profile on **LinkedIn**. This tool is considered the "most professional" of the social networks. Its Update field can be very strategic if used smartly. It is free and the "community" has at least 40 million other professionals involved. A very cool tool on this site is its ability to join *or create* special interest area groups.

   The free groups cover every possible interest area or niche. If you can't find the right one, you can create one and be its moderator. This is perhaps the easiest way for you to become a thought leader online. You simply serve as moderator for a very strategic group in your niche! I once created a group on LinkedIn, got too busy to do anything at all with it, and still ended up with nearly 50 people joining it!

2. **Facebook** is also an important place to have a presence. If one quarter of one percent of its 200 million+ users find you, you are in the money! FaceBook has been considered more social and "younger" but it is now emerging with thousands of interest groups, professional listings, businesses, fan groups and more. MySpace is similar to FaceBook in functionality and has a rep for being the home for more "creative types" (music, arts, and content). If that is your sector, stay with MySpace as it is very viable. Like LinkedIn, FaceBook

allows you to join or create your own special interest groups. This may cast a wider net for you due to the sheer numbers on FaceBook. One report said over half of FaceBook members live outside of the USA. What a global opportunity!

3. **Twitter** is becoming *the* way to find, be found, and be fresh online. I think I'll try to sell that motto to them ('Be Found & Be Fresh on Twitter' –or does that sound like a dating site?). With this tool, the sky is the limit with it for creative, current exposure *and* strategic search. This site may be a shortcut to having your own blog because you can make pithy comments without having to spend hours writing intelligent, lengthy pieces of content!

◻ The genius to Twitter is its ability to build your own "cult." Simply by clicking "Follow" on the profiles of the people who interest you, you can build a group that applies to you and your goals. You'll be able to follow and be followed by people who matter to you inside or outside of your industry or interest groups. You can follow most anyone and you don't have to prove to them that you know them or get their permission to follow them (unless they block you). And many of those whom you elect to follow will choose to follow you in return. Magical!

◻ This "Twitter thing" is here to stay I am guessing because some guy named Barack Obama used it masterfully recently to help him orchestrate a big career move. You may have heard something about it...

4. **Your personal blog**. A blog is a web log of your thoughts and gains you credibility over time. But, if you just got laid off last week and think laying down 2,000 words will get you several job offers, you are wrong. Blogs *are* a tool which can build *some* kind of reputation, but that result happens over *time*. Don't start a credible blog on a vocational topic to showcase your wisdom *unless you plan to spend at least two or three hours a week* on it for six months or more. Two years would be better!

▫ Blogs take good thought and good analysis. If you approach them casually and sporadically you will look casual and sporadic. The best bloggers are facilitators of a niche's dialog. Great bloggers post other peoples' ideas and content **always with full attribution.** Don't try too hard to look like *the* expert "know-it-all." Those kinds of kids got beat up on the playground. The online equivalent of that is the bully detractor/poster that can unravel your credibility with just a few keystrokes. Great bloggers include viable data and analysis on interesting topics that *matter* to their audiences.

▫ Good bloggers may get noticed by the traditional media or even just inside their own industry. But none of that happens overnight. A daily, *quality* post at the same time or a weekly one at the same time of day will typically build a following. There are books on how to get your blog noticed. Learn about them at **www.growmedia.com.**

**Wordpress.com and www.Blogger.com** are two of the more popular tools that host your personal blogs for free. These tools have amazing and simple features which allow you to be up and running with a professional looking blog in very little time. You just have to do the heavy lifting of creating the intelligent content. They provide the entire infrastructure you need. Blogosphere, here you come!

◻ Many people have created blogs which go on to become significant revenue generators! Visit grow-media.com to find links to books and stories about this.

5. **Your Own Website.** You can quite easily have your very own FREE, fully functioning web site via tools such as **www.tripod.lycos.com.** That one allows you to create a personal or small business web site at no cost. This gives you more features and more control than LinkedIn, FaceBook, Twitter, Wordpress, etc. offer since it is yours and dedicated to you. This tool and similar web hosting sites (including Yahoo Merchant Solutions) will also allow your small business to have ecommerce options and collect revenue.

◻ One downside of the *free* Tripod plan is that they tack their name into your URL (site name) after *your* name for your site. This makes it awkward if you are trying to build a brand around "your" site.

◻ Also, your site with them will have a banner ad at the top of your content. This is fine since they are hosting your site for free. Consider paying about $5 a month to them to have your own "clean" site name with no banner ads on it. Their site explains all this.

◻ www.Enom.com is also a good, full service, yet inexpensive host of web services. They have site-building templates, low costs, and excellent customer service where you can actually talk to a support people without an eternal wait! And when you are ready for your site to collect money from other people, they too have ecommerce plans which enable that.

This five point summary on how to build an online presence is simply that—a summary. Technology and online offerings change too fast for this to be a definitive list or a comprehensive industry profile. I am sure there are many tools out there which are excellent and I just haven't used them or heard about them. This book is about how to market your career and vocational background; the above tools, and the dozens of others similar to them can help you do just that. Remember...

## *Content is the Key!*

If you are trying to build a reputation, a career, a business or simply your professional network, get started now. Create or improve your online footprint in the social media space because these tools are revolutionizing business and relationships. Major corporations are working to set up their own similar tools in-house to facilitate employee communication and engagement.

You can use these tools at any level...create a professional quality, 30-minute video that leaves them breathless, or you can invest 15 minutes creating or improving a simple LinkedIn profile. Either way, pay attention to Nike and "Just Do It!"

### Let me know if I can help!

# About Americas Job Coach

Paul David Madsen has been involved in all facets of the talent procurement and promotion sector since 1984. He has worked in key roles for two multi-billion dollar information-technology consulting corporations, the corporate office of a mid-market insurance corporation, and several local and regional executive search, staffing, contracting, and placement companies in various niches. Paul has:

- Made over 25,000 headhunting, recruiting, sourcing, screening, and interviewing contacts with active and passive job seekers in numerous states and countries.

- Conducted thousands of sales calls and candidate pitch presentations to hiring managers and human resources professionals at corporations of all sizes; also, he has worked on the other side of the desk as as an in-house human resources recruiter for several firms.

- Placed hundreds of professionals into new corporate positions across the USA.

- Read, evaluated, and written tens of thousands of candidate resumes over 2.5 decades.

- Has "been branded" as America's Job Coach since 2001 and hosted "Career Repair On the Air*" –a call-in talk radio show, in addition to numerous job coaching appearances on local, regional, and national radio and television.

- Taught career transition seminars (since 1992) to over 1,000 attendees with backgrounds including early retirees, victims of lay-offs and outsourcing, new college grads, and professionals who have been fired, burned-out, or were just restless with their work.

- Founded two executive recruiting firms, growmedia.com and held profit and loss responsibility for a national, publicly held staffing company.

- Authored *Laid Off & Loving It (2001 edition), Laid Off & Loving It For 2010,* a "future classic" novel, several career transition-related seminars.

- Earned his Certified Personnel Consultant (CPC) designation from the National Association of Personnel Services in 1987.

- Graduated from Dana College in Nebraska and lives in that state with his wife and three children.

# Services Offered by America's Job Coach

**America's Job Coach adds value to these people:**

A. **Executives and Senior Level employees** who have reached the upper levels of their field or careers.

B. **Intermediate Level** employees who are established in their work histories but are not done "climbing the ladder."

C. **Emerging professionals** who are "up and comers" or just starting and defining their careers.

D. **Small business entrepreneurs** who are planning *or running* their own smaller ventures (except in the IT consulting/contracting space)

**Coaching is delivered via these vehicles:**

◻ Small groups in a live seminar format

◻ Online webinars (recorded and live both in audio and video versions)

◻ Virtual (phone, SKYPE, text messages, email)

◻ One-on-one meetings in the Omaha, NE area only (limited availability)

# Most Popular Services of America's Job Coach

**(For pricing please visit www.americasjobcoach.com)**

**1. TwitterVator Speech Creation:**

The hardest part of writing a book is creating a strategic back-cover *summary* of it. This book tells how to create your own TwitterVator Speech, but some people may still want a little help to create a great summary in 140 characters or less. I can create a great one for you (guaranteed) for a *surprisingly* low investment. I do this over the phone or online and it usually takes about an hour or less of your time.

**2. Resume/Cover Letter Services:**

There is still a need for resumes and cover letters (or cover paragraphs) because most employers require the completion of an online job application form filled out and accompanied by an attached or pasted resume.

Don't skimp on this still-important document! Most HR departments retain the "legal" online application in their systems and then forward the applicant's resume to the hiring manager who makes a decision about you based on that. A resume might get 15 seconds of fame so doesn't it make sense to have the best, expertly prepared document possible?

**A. Full-Boat Resume Preparation:**

◻ This is just like it sounds—the full boat deal of a top-to-bottom creation, reinvention, remodeling, or a makeover of what you have done in your career. Your resume will emerge as a stellar, persuasive document of your career history and something you'll be proud to use to market yourself (guaranteed).

- ▢ I'll need up to an hour or two of your time (depending upon the complexity of your career history) to interview you in person or by phone. I'll build on and improve whatever information you already have regarding the documentation of your career.

- ▢ This process is done by phone, Skype email, or in person.

- ▢ This content is usable on various social media tools!

- ▢ Satisfaction guaranteed!

**B. Your Resume TWEAK:**

- ▢ Your existing resume is likely *OK* since you have worked hard on it, tweaked it, been to seminars about it, and have even read books about it.

- ▢ But, *is* there one little 'gotcha' that you are just too close to see? Employers get STACKS of resumes everyday, so use my quick Resume Tweak to possibly make a difference. Put an extra set of expert eyes to work for you!

- ▢ Simply email me your pasted document or tell me where to see it online. Within 20 minutes (from when *I* start on it) you'll have my expert opinion about any potential changes that you *should* make. This costs less than a big lunch for you and a friend at a nice restaurant, but buys you some great peace of mind.

◻ This process is all done by email or web-based written communication.

## 3. Interview Preparation/Practice and Offer Negotiation Strategies

◻ They called and you have an **interview scheduled** with a hot potential employer! Yeah! Emotions are high! *Don't blow this critical opportunity* for a better income without first consulting with American's Job Coach.

◻ An interview is **not** an offer, and employers have dozens of good candidates these days. America's Job Coach has prepared hundreds of people for successful interviews. Be ready for interview "gotchas." You can engage this placement expert to help and an hour of practice is a very worthwhile way to help you set yourself apart from your competition.

◻ Regarding negotiation: You are waiting for an offer and wonder about negotiation. There is a lot of emotion and tension here too so it may be important to bring in an expert. You use an attorney and a tax expert and a doctor and insurance professional...why not use America's Job Coach (who has negotiated hundreds of job offers) to help?

◻ Interview prep = Individual Sessions are one or two hours in length

- Negotiation prep = Individual Sessions are 30 or 60 minutes in length
- These sessions are conducted by phone, Skype, or in person

To get the latest updates on these and other services offered by America's Job Coach, please contact:

**services@americasjobcoach.com**

*Service offerings are limited and pricing is subject to change at any time.*

# Acknowledgments / Gratitude

The stories you have read are a blend of the thousands of people I have interviewed (by phone and in person), taught in seminars, researched, individually coached, screened for and/or enrolled in college, recruited, and placed in new positions. They have formed the backdrop of this book and special thanks go out to one seminar attendee in particular: Meg N. "insisted" that I put my seminar content into a book.

More appreciation goes out to my "support staff" who each contributed to this project in their own unique way: Curt M, Gary J, Jackie P, Joe B, Verlan H, Dave K, Helga H, Barbara K, Wayne M, and my title selection focus group. Also special thanks to the proofing, layout, and editing efforts of Mary H, and Mark K, and Verlan H. And thanks for the the dedication and patience of Pat Rasch at www.bookandcoverdesign.com. People do judge a book by its cover and you did great!

"Inspirational gratitude" again goes to Lester L. Madsen and this 2010 edition is dedicated to the memory of Laura L. Sumpter who was a "career coach" and much, much more to many people.

Lastly, my content projects are completed at a cost of unavailability to my wife and children. Thanks to Lisa, Laura, Dane, and Jake for your patience and support—together we are adding value to others!

*9780971383616*